Teachings on Sakya Pandita's
Clarifying the Sage's Intent

This book is based on teachings given by Venerable Khenchen Appey Rinpoche at Sakya Tenphel Ling, Singapore, in 1986. The text was originally translated and edited by Venerable Ngawang Samten Choephel. It was later extensively revised in 2005 at the International Buddhist Academy, Kathmandu, by Pauline Westwood, under the guidance of Khenpo Jamyang Tenzin. This text was edited for publication in 2007 by Emma Cobb.

Mahayana (*theg pa chen po*)
In terms of the doctrine and tenets, Mahayana refers to the teachings of the 'higher vehicles,' or the upper two of the four Indian Buddhist tenets. In terms of causes and results, it refers to the paths and results of bodhisattvas.

Maudgalaputra (*mchog tu gyur pa*)
With Shariputra, one of the two main contemporary (shravaka) disciples of Buddha. He was reputed to possess highly developed miraculous powers.

Mimamsa (*dpyod pa ba*)
One of the Indian Hindu philosophical schools which asserts that the Hindu scriptures are self-originated and that the 'self' is permanent and partless.

Nagarjuna (*klu grub*)
Nagarjuna was a great Buddhist master born about four hundred years after the passing of Shakyamuni Buddha. He wrote fundamental texts on all three Dharma Wheels. He is particularly noted for his works expounding the Mahayana and for his foundational expositions on the Madhyamika (Middle Way) philosophy.

nagas (klu)
Creatures usually with a serpent-like appearance, classified as animals, who control ponds and rivers.

nirvana (*mya ngan las 'das pa*)
Literally, this means 'gone beyond suffering.' Philosophical texts use this term mainly to refer to the result of extinguishing samsaric cause and result.

Nyingma (*rnying ma*)
One of the four principal schools of Tibetan Buddhism; known as the 'old translation' school.

obscuration of defilements (*nyon mongs pa'i sgrib pa*)
This obscuration consists of all the mental and emotional defilements and their seeds, which block the practitioner from achieving liberation from samsara.

obscuration of phenomena (*shes bya'i sgrib pa*)
This is the more subtle obscuration which blocks the practitioner from achieving Buddhahood. It consists of the

manifested conceptual thoughts (other than defilements) and the residues of manifested obscuration of defilements and obscuration of phenomena.

Paramitayana *(rgyu pha rol tu phyin pa'i theg pa)*
Also known as Sutrayana, this refers to the 'causal' Mahayana as distinct from the 'resultant' Vajrayana.

pratimoksha vow *(so sor thar pa'i sdom pa)*
Individually liberating vow.

Pratyekabuddhayana *(rang rgyal theg pa)*
The paths of the Buddhist spiritual practitioners which aim to attain 'self-conquered Buddhahood' and their results, the qualities of realization possessed by 'self-conquered arhats.'

Sakya *(sa skya)*
One of the four principal schools of Tibetan Buddhism.

Samantabhadra *(kun tu bzang po)*
A bodhisattva who was one of the eight great closer sons of Buddha Shakyamuni.

samatha *(zhi gnas)*
Also known as calm abiding. This refers to a mental state resting one-pointedly on the virtuous object, pacified of conceptual thought of signs or elaborations. It is a prerequisite to evoking and practising vipashyana (or special insight) meditation.

seven branches or limbs of enlightenment *(byang chub kyi yan lag bdun)*
These consist of mindfulness, wisdom, effort, joy, pliancy, concentration and equanimity, each of which is combined with the understanding of the lack of inherent existence of all phenomena.

Shakra
See **Indra**

Shariputra
With Maudgalaputra, one of the two main contemporary disciples of Buddha. Among the Shravaka disciples, he was reputed to have the most excellent discerning wisdom.

Sutra (*mdo*)
The original discourses of Buddha apart from the Tantric teachings. They are divided into three pitakas, or baskets.

the three factors (*'khor gsum*)
In the context of activities, the doer, the object and the deed.

the three realms (*khams gsum*)
These are sometimes known as the 'three spheres' to distinguish them from the six realms of the desire realm. The three realms, which include all sentient beings in samsaric existence, are the desire realm, the form realm and the formless realm. The first consists of the six classes of habitats and inhabitants: hell beings, hungry ghosts, animals, humans, demi-gods and gods. The latter two are more subtle realms populated by beings who have achieved certain states of meditative absorption.

tirthikas (*mu stegs rtag*)
Heretics; non-Buddhist philosophers.

Tripitaka (*sde snod gsum*)
The three 'baskets' of Buddha's teachings: Vinaya pitaka (*'dul ba sde snod*), consisting of teachings mainly on morality; Sutra pitaka (*mdo sde'i sde snod*), teachings mainly on meditative concentration; and Abhidharma pitaka (*mngon pa'i sde snod*), teachings mainly on wisdom.

twelve elements
The six sense objects (outer sources of perception) and the six senses (inner sources of perception).

two truths (*bden gnyis*)
Relative truth (*kun rdzob kyi bden pa*) and ultimate truth (*don dam pa'i bden pa*). Relative truth, also known as conventional truth, is the truth perceived by beings with ordinary minds. This varies from one species to another. Ultimate truth is what is directly perceived by an arya during meditative equipoise. Philosophy texts also refer to 'ultimate truth established through logical proofs.' This is known as 'simulated' ultimate truth, explained from a perspective of relative truth.

universal emperor (*'khor lo sgyur ba'i rgyal po*)
Chakravartin, world ruler, universal ruler.

Vajrayana (*rgyud*)

The branch of Mahayana which advocates secret Tantric practices as the greater skilful means for attaining Buddhahood in the shortest possible period of time. It is also referred to as the 'resultant' Mahayana (as distinct from the 'causal' Mahayana).

Vinaya (*'dul ba*)

The moral teachings of Buddha; the first of the three baskets of the Tripitaka.

yidam (*yi dam*)

Personal tutelary or meditational deity. The yidam is the means for attainment by practitioners who have been initiated into the deity's practice.

Teachings on Sakya Pandita's

Clarifying
the Sage's Intent

Khenchen Appey Rinpoche

Vajra Publications
www.vajrabooks.com.np

Teachings on Sakya Pandita's *Clarifying the Sages Intent*,
by Khenchen Appey Rinpoche at Sakya Tenphel Ling,
Singapore, 1986

Published by

Vajra Publications
Jyatha, Thamel, P.O. Box 21779, Kathmandu, Nepal
Tel.: 977-1-4220562, Fax: 977-1-4246536
e-mail: bidur_la@mos.com.np
www.vajrabooks.com.np

Distributor

Vajra Book Shop
Kathmandu, Nepal

First published in Kathmandu, 2001
Second revised edition, 2008

ISBN 978-9937-506-24-3

Printed in Nepal

Table of Contents

Venerable Khenchen Appey Rinpoche

Khenchen Appey Rinpoche received his training in philosophic and literary studies under such highly esteemed scholars as Dagyab Lodro, the Dzongsar seminary master. He received instruction on the profound Vajrayana teachings from many great masters, including Jamyang Khyentse Chokyi Lodro and Dezhung Ajam Rinpoche. He taught in several seminaries in Tibet and India and founded the renowned Sakya College, near Rajpur, Dehra Dun, in India.

After moving to Nepal, Rinpoche began the work of establishing the International Buddhist Academy (IBA) in Kathmandu, which opened in 2001. It is dedicated to making the great tradition of rigorous Buddhist scholarship and soundly based practice available to students from all over the world.

Foreword

My purpose in reissuing this text, based on teachings I gave in 1986 at Sakya Tenphel Ling in Singapore, is to present the entire teaching of *Clarifying the Sage's Intent* by Sakya Pandita in a simple format which can be easily understood by people from diverse backgrounds. Though the coverage is brief, it nevertheless includes the complete meaning or essence of the entire teaching. *Clarifying the Sage's Intent* encapsulates the intended meaning of the teachings Lord Buddha gave to the world. It is also known by two other titles: 'Describing the very· pure path of the bodhisattva, or the path to enlightenment' and 'The book taught to large gatherings of people.' The latter title reflects the fact that when Sakya Pandita travelled throughout Tibet and China, this was the text he taught most often.

Clarifying the Sage's Intent describes the stages of the bodhisattva path from the very beginning right up to full and perfect enlightenment, following the teaching tradition of the great early Kadampas. The teachings are based on two verses from Maitreya's *Mahayanasutralamkara* (Ornament of the Sutras), which cover the entire Mahayana teachings of the Buddha. *Mahayanasutralamkara* expounds ten stages of practice. The first is spiritual propensity; the second is convinced adherence to religion; the third is generating the enlightenment thought; the fourth is accomplishing the perfections of generosity and the remaining perfections; the fifth is maturing sentient beings; the sixth is entering upon the stainless paths; the seventh is thoroughly purifying the realms, the eighth is nonabiding nirvana; the ninth is the highest awakening and the tenth is demonstration. The first of these, spiritual propensity, is the foundation for practice. The next six stages consist of the path and how to accomplish it. The last three stages are the results of the path. In common with all Mahayana teachings, it contains three aspects:

foundation, path and result. Sakya Pandita firmly maintained that a thorough grounding achieved by studying the texts, based on the correct practice of morality, is the essential prerequisite for commencing sitting meditation practices. It is therefore extremely important for us to understand the teachings and contemplate their meaning. Only in this way will we be able to meditate successfully and gain direct realizations.

It is my hope that these teachings will help students of Dharma to progress along the path successfully, gain higher rebirths and ultimately attain the fruit of full enlightenment.

Kathmandu, 2008

Khenchen Appey

Sakya Pandita

The great master Sakya Pandita was one of the five founding masters of the Sakya school of Tibetan Buddhism. It is said that through his practice of Vajrayana guruyoga, he attained the first bhumi during his lifetime. From then onwards he gained increasingly higher realizations. Considered to be the greatest scholar ever to have appeared in Tibet, Sakya Pandita is believed to be an emanation of the Bodhisattva Manjushri. Among his many accomplishments, he mastered the five major sciences, which include arts and crafts, medicine, Sanskrit, logic and Buddhist philosophy, and the five minor sciences of poetry, synonyms, lexicography, astrology, dance and drama, which he studied with eminent Indian scholars. Although there were many esteemed scholars in Tibet prior to the birth of Sakya Pandita, no others had ever mastered both the five major and the five minor sciences. He wrote many works on Buddhist philosophy and on other aspects of the major and minor sciences, and established teachings on them in Tibet. Some of his works were even translated into Sanskrit, as his reputation extended far beyond the borders of the Snow Land. He was held in such high esteem that on one occasion, six Hindu scholars travelled all the way to Tibet to debate with him. Sakya Pandita defeated all of them.

'Pandita' is an Indian title reserved for scholars learned in both Dharma and in worldly knowledge and skills. Sakya Pandita was the first Tibetan to be honoured with this title, which was bestowed on him by his master, Shakya Shribhadra, in recognition of his outstanding erudition, which spanned all fields of study. Because of his vast and profound mastery of Sanskrit, Sakya Pandita could translate into Tibetan entirely on his own without assistance from Indian masters. He was the first Tibetan translator to do so (later on, of course, other Tibetan translators followed in his footsteps). He was also the first Tibetan to propagate Buddhist teachings beyond the borders of Tibet. During the period of Mongol rule in China, a minor Mongol emperor named Gho-dhen invited him to teach the Holy Dharma in Mongolia. According to Mongolian historical accounts, Sachen Kunga Nyingpo, the first founder of the Sakya lineage, had been invited previously. These sources mention that although Sachen had been unable to go himself, his grandson, Sakya Pandita, travelled there in later years and gave Dharma teachings throughout the length and breadth of Mongolia. Both Mongolian and Chinese sources refer to Sakya Pandita's arrival and to his success in introducing Buddhist teachings.

When Sakya Pandita first arrived in Mongolia, the Mongolian language had no script. Sakya Pandita actually devised the Mongolian alphabet, which was subsequently revised by later scholars. This enabled the entire Buddhist canon (i.e. the Tripitaka, the Indian commentarial teachings and other Tibetan teachings) to be translated into the Mongolian language from Tibetan.

According to Tibetan history, Buddhism actually reached China before Sakya Pandita's arrival. In fact it is recorded that teachings had begun to appear there as early as 110 years after the parinirvana of Shakyamuni Buddha. Over time, both Hinayana and Mahayana teachings were taught. It is said that many followers of the Hinayana tradition gained the various stages of the arya's realization, and many followers of the Mahayana tradition accomplished advanced bodhisattva practices, such as giving their bodies to others and so on. With regard to Vajrayana, a small number of the lower Tantras had reached China, although it appears that none of the higher Tantras were taught there prior to Sakya Pandita's arrival. It therefore appears that Sakya Pandita was instrumental in introducing major Vajrayana teachings to China and propagating them widely throughout the empire. His pioneering work was later continued by his nephew, Chogyal Phagpa, who gave the Hevajra initiation to Kublai Khan. It was largely through the efforts of Sakya Pandita and Chogyal Phagpa that the Mahayana and Vajrayana teachings took root in China. Chogyal Phagpa was appointed personal teacher to the emperor and was thus in a key position to disseminate the teachings. It is recorded that on one occasion he taught to an assembly of seventy thousand monks. However, following the demise of Chogyal Phagpa, the influence of the Sakya tradition began to wane, not only in China but also in Tibet. At this time the Kagyud tradition reached pre-eminence, until it in turn declined when the Gelug tradition rose to prominence.

The biographies relate that, prior to his passing away, Sakya Pandita displayed the excellent marks, including the protuberance on the crown of the head and the tuft of hair between the eyebrows, following the example of Buddha Shakyamuni and great masters such as Nagarjuna.

1

Buddha Nature

This is the first of the ten stages of practice expounded in the *Mahayanasutralamkara*. We can define 'Buddha nature' or 'spiritual propensity' as the natural cause of Buddhahood, which all sentient beings have possessed from beginningless time. The developed Buddha nature or spiritual propensity, on the other hand, is present only in those who have produced the thought of awakening. We might say that the natural Buddha nature or spiritual propensity is the 'support,' while the developed Buddha nature or spiritual propensity is the 'supported.'

In order to practise Mahayana, one's Buddha nature must first be awakened into the Mahayana race. There are four signs to indicate that this has occurred:

(1) Possessing great compassion from the beginning, even before commencing practice.
(2) Having faith in the Three Jewels.[1]
(3) Being patient towards harm done by others.
(4) Possessing a natural inclination to perform virtuous deeds.

There are four impairments to the awakening of the 'race' within us. These are:

---

1 The Three Jewels, also known as the Triple Gem, are Buddha, Dharma (the holy teachings, including realization and analytical cessation) and Sangha (spiritual assembly).

(i)   Being completely under the power of defilements. In other words, our actions are driven by afflictive emotions such as desire, anger and ignorance. In this situation, the thought of practising Dharma does not arise.

(ii) Being under the evil influence of bad friends and teachers. Under such influence, we cannot turn our mind towards spiritual practice. A false teacher who preaches the wrong path leads us away from the true teaching and prevents us from turning to other teachers who teach the true Dharma.

(iii) Being poor. This means being obstructed from entering the Dharma through lack of adequate food, clothing, shelter or other basic necessities.

(iv) Being under the power of others. This means lacking independence to think freely. A great Indian scholar once remarked that when a person is young, he is under the power of his parents and is not allowed to think for himself; when he grows up, he comes under the power of his wife; and when he is old, he comes under the power of his children and grandchildren. Thus one is never truly free to do as one wishes.

Severed Buddha nature

There are some beings whose spiritual propensity has been temporarily severed. There are four principal categories of beings in this situation:

(i)   those who lack virtue conducive to enlightenment;

(ii) those who perform only misconduct;

(iii) those who have spoiled the seed of positive factors; and

(iv) those who possess the seed, but have not ripened it through performing virtuous deeds.

The various Buddhist traditions have different ways of interpreting this concept of spiritual propensity. For example, the Cittamatrin (Mind-Only) school teaches that there are four types of race. With regard to the first three races, one may belong to the race of shravakas, the race of pratyekabuddhas or the race of Mahayana. In addition, they claim, there is also a fourth race consisting of living beings whose Buddha nature has been permanently severed and who therefore can never attain any form of enlightenment. However, the Madhyamika (Middle Way) school does not accept the proposition that there are beings whose Buddha nature has been permanently severed. Furthermore, this school teaches that although beings may belong temporarily to the race of shravakas or pratyekabuddhas, all beings will ultimately enter the final path to Buddhahood. Nevertheless, since the Madhyamika school believes that cyclic existence is endless, this is tantamount to accepting that some beings will never escape from it.

There are two stories to illustrate the point about the difficulty of awakening Buddha nature. The first concerns Angulimala, whose name means 'the one who wears the garland of fingers.' These events occurred when Buddha Shakyamuni was residing in Shravasti. At that time there was a great scholar living there who had a great many disciples. One day the king summoned this scholar to his palace. Before setting off on his journey, the scholar left behind one of his main disciples to guard his house and keep watch over his wife. At that time, this disciple was known as 'the one who is pleasing to look at,' because he was extremely handsome. Indeed, he was so good-looking that the scholar's wife became very attracted to him. In fact, when her husband and his other students had left, she approached the disciple in a very provocative manner. But the disciple refused to have anything to do with her. He explained that he thought of her as a mother and then ran away to escape her advances. The scholar's wife was mortified by this rejection, so she devised a plan to take revenge on the boy. She ripped her clothes to shreds, scratched her entire body and beat herself with a stick. When her husband returned, she told him that his young disciple had attacked her during his absence. The scholar believed his wife's story and decided to punish the boy by ruining his life. However, as this student was very clever, the teacher knew he would need to use considerable cunning. So he told the boy that he had forfeited his brahmin caste because of his bad behaviour. Furthermore, he said that unless he regained his status by killing a thousand human beings, he would never be able to attain liberation or be reborn in the heavenly realms. At first the boy refused, because he could not believe it would be right to kill people. However, by explaining that he must heed the words of his teacher who was instructing him in the correct understanding of the of the world's ways, his teacher eventually convinced him.

Having finally accepted his teacher's advice, the student set about the task he had been allotted. When he had succeeded in killing one thousand people, he reported back to his teacher. But the master told him he needed to produce proof of these killings. He told him he should cut a finger from the hand of each of the people he had killed, string these fingers together to make a garland and wear the garland around his neck. He would therefore have to kill another thousand people in order to collect this proof. So the boy set out again. Because of the necklace of fingers around his neck, he acquired the name 'Angulimala.'

At the time when he had succeeded in killing a further 999 people, Angulimala saw his mother, who had become alarmed by his long absence and had left her house to search for him. When the boy saw his mother approaching, he decided to kill her. This would both complete the goal of a thousand victims and enable him gain the state of rebirth in a heavenly realm. Furthermore, by killing his mother, he reasoned, he would be placing her into the heavenly realms also. With such thoughts in mind, he drew out his knife and began to approach her.

Through his omniscience, Buddha Shakyamuni perceived what was happening. He saw that this was the right moment to awaken the boy and place him on the path to cessation. So Buddha began to walk towards him. The boy noticed the wondrous figure of Buddha coming his way and called out to him to stop. He asked Buddha who he was to have the audacity to walk towards him like that. Buddha replied that he was the Fully Awakened One. He continued approaching. Angulimala shouted out to Buddha that he would kill him unless he stopped. Buddha replied that he was actually standing still, not moving. He said that he always remained still in a place where no one would ever harm anyone else. Angulimala should also abide in that place, where he would have the patience never to harm another living being.

Buddha explained to Angulimala that he had allowed himself to be completely misled to the point of wanting to kill his own mother, who with great kindness and compassion had come to help him. He told Angulimala he had been tricked into following a false path, which would lead only to enormous suffering. Thus Buddha tamed

Angulimala's mind and convinced him he was on the wrong path. Upon hearing these words, Angulimala there and then took refuge in Buddha and requested ordination. Buddha agreed, and Angulimala was ordained. Through Buddha's teachings, which had awakened his seed of virtue, Angulimala would later attain arhatship within that same lifetime.

It is said that at one time Angulimala ascended into the sky and flew to the city of Kosala. When he arrived, King Prasenajit was in the process of preparing his army to hunt Angulimala down and kill him because of his past misdeeds. When the soldiers saw Angulimala coming down towards them from the sky, they were terrified. They ran off to tell the king that Angulimala had arrived. At that point, the king asked Buddha's advice. Buddha told him Angulimala had attained arhatship and was no longer a threat to anyone. The king wondered why, since Buddha's power was great enough to help Angulimala attain arhatship, he had not restrained him from killing all those people in the first place. Buddha responded by referring to the five hundred servants who were working for the king as bird hunters. He asked the king why he did not stop them from killing birds, since he had the power to do so. The king saw the point of Buddha's question and immediately ordered the bird hunters to stop killing birds from then on, or face the penalty of death for breaking his command. For their part, the five hundred bird hunters met together and agreed that although they would have to obey the king's order, it did not apply to their sons. So they ordered their sons to go out and kill the birds instead of them. In other words, since they belonged to the race of slaughterers, they were unable to relinquish this nonvirtuous behaviour. Others could do nothing to restrain them from committing nonvirtuous actions, and hence their race could not be awakened. However, it is said that later on Buddha manifested miraculously in front of them and gave them a teaching. As a result, they were able to correct their thinking, give up killing and prevent their sons from further killing. From this account we can see that it is possible for the race to be awakened through the kindness of Buddha. However, it appears that there are many people who do not have the power to awaken their Buddha nature through their own efforts.

The second story is about a young Chinese boy, whose family one day decided to send him to a temple which housed many holy images, including statues of the Buddha and the Bodhisattva Avalokiteshvara. He was told to study these images closely and learn to identify them. However, he didn't want to. In fact, he felt strong aversion towards all holy images. So before entering the temple, he put on a blindfold to make sure he would not catch even a glimpse of any of the images. No matter how much his parents urged him, he flatly refused to look at them. Later on, his parents thought of a plan to get around their son's obstinacy. They tried placing an image of Bodhisattva Avalokiteshvara inside a vessel, which they covered and placed before him. Without telling him what it contained, they instructed him to open the vessel and look at the image inside it. However, their son was suspicious and became annoyed. He wrapped a length of cloth around his eyes and ears so he would not be able either to see or to hear. Wrapping another cloth around his hand, he picked up the vessel and threw it away. This story is another illustration of how difficult it is for us to awaken our race.

With regard to the etymology of the term 'Buddha nature,' 'spiritual propensity' or 'race,' the Sanskrit word is *gotra*. With respect to the first syllable of this word, *go*, if we change the *o* to *u* and add *na*, we have the word *guna*, which means 'excellent qualities.' Then with the second syllable, if we divide the syllable *tra* into its components, the result is *tara*, which means 'liberating.' Therefore, as one is liberated on the basis of excellent qualities, Buddha nature or spiritual propensity may be described as the 'excellent liberating quality.'

2

Producing the Aspiration to Engage in Buddha's Teachings

The second of the ten stages of practice expounded in the *Mahayanasutralamkara* is 'convinced adherence to religion.' This refers to taking refuge. In order to produce the aspiration to engage in Buddha's teachings, we must first understand the teachings on taking refuge. When we take refuge, we affirm our trust in the Triple Gem, the objects of taking refuge, and in the shrine embodying them. The presentation on taking refuge has four topics:

(1) the nature of taking refuge;
(2) the divisions of taking refuge and their differentiation;
(3) the precepts of taking refuge; and
(4) the benefits of taking refuge.

(1) The nature of taking refuge

The definition of taking refuge is 'affirming our reliance on the highest objects of refuge.' In other words, when we take refuge, we promise sincerely, from the very depths of our being, to place our reliance in the Triple Gem, the most excellent of all refuges.

(2) The divisions of taking refuge and their differentiation

This has three main categories:

- taking worldly refuge, which is the refuge taken by ordinary beings;

- taking Hinayana refuge; and
- taking Mahayana refuge.

Each of these may be further subdivided into two parts. Taking worldly refuge is categorized from the viewpoint of the object of taking refuge and the mind which takes refuge; taking Hinayana refuge is categorized into taking Shravakayana refuge and taking Pratyekabuddhayana refuge; and taking Mahayana refuge is divided into taking Paramitayana refuge and taking Vajrayana refuge. When we examine these three categories of taking refuge, we will see that each has different causes. The causes of taking worldly refuge are fear of the sufferings of cyclic existence and faith in mundane or supramundane objects. With regard to the Hinayana, the causes are similar to the causes of the worldlings, except that the emphasis is on faith in the Triple Gem. With regard to the Mahayana, although fear of cyclic existence and faith in the Triple Gem are present, the principal cause for taking refuge is the great compassion. Compassion may be defined as the wish for sentient beings to be free from sufferings. All Mahayana practices begin with a meditation on compassion.

When we refer to taking worldly refuge from the viewpoint of object, this means taking refuge in worldly deities such as Brahma or Indra, or in lower worldly entities such as local spirits. Of course those who take refuge in such objects cannot be classed as Buddhists, and this refuge does not lead to any of the liberations. When we speak of worldly refuge-taking from the viewpoint of the mind, this refers to those who, despite the fact that they take refuge in the Triple Gem, do so motivated either by fear of the sufferings of this and future lives, or by the wish to gain benefits in this life and future lives. This type of refuge-taking does not lead to any of the liberations, either.

Although both Hinayana and Mahayana take the Triple Gem as their objects of refuge, they interpret the characteristics of the Triple Gem in different ways. For example, Hinayana followers maintain that Buddha has only two bodies, the Dharmakaya and the Rupakaya, whereas the followers of Mahayana believe that Buddha has three bodies: the Dharmakaya, the Sambhogakaya and the Nirmanakaya. Within the Hinayana tradition, taking refuge in Buddha means affirming Buddha as the teacher who shows the path to liberation; taking refuge in the Dharma refers to affirming only the path leading to cessation; and taking refuge in the Sangha refers to affirming ordinary ordained people who have renounced the world and those who show the path of the four noble truths as one's spiritual companions. According to Mahayana, taking refuge in Buddha means to affirm the one possessing the three bodies of enlightenment as the teacher; taking refuge in Dharma means affirming the Mahayana teachings and the realizations gained on the bodhisattva path as the actual path; and taking refuge in the Sangha refers to affirming specifically those who have attained the arya bodhisattva bhumis as spiritual companions on the path to enlightenment.

With regard to time span, this also depends on the three categories of refuge takers. The worldly take refuge from the present moment until they accomplish their short-lived purposes, whether these be material objects of desire or mundane qualities such as fame, position, financial success or some other benefit. Taking refuge through such motivation is not a basis for spiritual practice; it is not the path leading to liberation. Within the Hinayana, one takes refuge from this time until one dies; in other words, for the duration of the present life. In Mahayana, we take refuge from this time forth until we reach the stage of perfect and complete enlightenment. With regard to the purpose of taking refuge, the worldly person takes refuge in order to overcome his fears and to accomplish his desires. The Hinayana practitioner takes refuge for the purpose of gaining personal liberation. The Mahayana practitioner takes refuge in order to gain perfect and complete Buddhahood, for the purpose of leading all sentient beings to enlightenment.

(3) The precepts of taking refuge

There are two categories of precepts for taking refuge: the general precepts and the individual precepts. The general precepts relate to the Triple Gem as a whole, whereas the individual precepts relate to each of the individual Gems.

(i) The general precepts of taking refuge

(a) The first general precept is always to accompany those who are holy

This means that one who has taken refuge in the Triple Gem should stay close to a teacher who has attained some degree of accomplishment and should associate with those who are also practising the Dharma. If one is unable to live in a spiritual community, one should try to associate with people who can help one to maintain virtue.

(b) The second general precept is to listen to the teachings and to study the Dharma

In other words, we must not listen in a haphazard way to just any kind of teaching. We should very carefully study the proper teachings of Buddha, whether they be Hinayana, Mahayana or Vajrayana. We must study the teachings belonging to the Tripitaka: Vinaya, Sutra and Abhidharma. One who has received Vajrayana initiation should also study the Tantric scriptures. Although it is very difficult to study Buddha's teachings in the Sutra form, because they are not systematized, we should study the treatises by later masters such as Nagarjuna, Maitreya, Asanga, Dharmakirti and so on. These treatises expound the Sutras in an excellent manner, to enable followers to understand Buddha's direct words. Those who engage in the study of the Tantric teachings, which are very complex and difficult to understand, should carefully follow the various explanatory teachings by great adepts such as Birwapa (Virupa), Indrabhuti and Drilbuba and so on, who wrote very clear explanations about them. Sakya Pandita stated that if a teaching has the following six qualities, we can trust that we are hearing the genuine teaching of Buddha:

(1) Buddha himself must have taught it;
(2) it must come within the teachings systematized by the various Buddhist councils;
(3) great scholars and adepts must have commented on it;
(4) great Indian saints or Mahasiddhas must have meditated upon it;

(5) great translators must have translated it from the Indian languages to other languages, such as Tibetan; and

(6) all the great Buddhist scholars must have known and accepted it.

If a teaching is endowed with these six qualities, we can accept it as the authentic teaching of Buddha. Though other schools may also have produced positive teachings, they do not lead us to the right result. We should not, therefore, study them or meditate on them.

(c) The third general precept is that we must practise the Buddhist teachings according to what Buddha taught
Morality is the very basis for spirituality. In order to practise morality properly, we must rely on the Vinaya, Buddha's teachings on morality, to train our body, voice and mind in appropriate ways. In order to develop meditative absorption, we must rely on the Sutra teachings. In order to engage in the training on wisdom, we must rely on the Abhidharma teachings. This applies to both Hinayana and Mahayana practitioners. Those who practise Vajrayana should in addition swallow and digest the various teachings of the Tantras in order to understand and practise them properly. Before we engage in any daily activity, we need to direct our mind towards the Triple Gem and receive their blessings. Before we set out to go anywhere, we should think of whichever Buddha of the five Buddha families resides in the direction we are taking. By praying to that Buddha and seeking his blessings, we can accomplish whatever we set out to do without hindrances or obstacles. For example, if we are going to a certain place within our own district, we should pray to Buddha Vairochana and seek his blessings; if we are heading east, we should pray to Buddha Akshobya; if we are heading south, we should pray to Buddha Ratnasambhava; if we are heading west, we should pray to Buddha Amitabha; and if we are heading north, we should pray to Buddha Amoghasiddhi.

Whenever we eat or drink, it is important to offer the first portion to the Triple Gem. There are many different ways to do this. For example, we can recite particular verses from the Sutras, or offer actual food to various spirits, as prescribed in the Vinaya teachings. There is a story of a demoness (Hariti, or Trog-ma in Tibetan) who used to eat children. It is said that in order to satisfy her, Buddha promised that henceforward his followers would offer a portion of their food to her. While eating, we should transform the way we perceive our food. For example, according to the Hinayana tradition, we may reflect that we are taking the food to keep our body healthy and maintain it as a vessel to practise the Dharma path. According to certain Mahayana traditions, since there are many different creatures living inside us, we should take the food not for ourselves alone, but also to nourish these creatures. Offering them food is a virtuous deed.

We should transform our sleep into the path of Dharma. We can do this by lying down in the lion position adopted by Buddha Shakyamuni while he passed away. When we are about to go to sleep, we should visualize that we are entering into the state of Dharmakaya. We should pray, 'May all sentient beings also attain the state of Dharmakaya.' When we awaken in the morning, we should pray, 'May all sentient beings attain the Rupakaya, or the noble form of Buddha.' In such ways we can transform both our waking and our sleeping activities into the path of Dharma.

Irrespective of whether we experience happiness or suffering in this life, we must never abandon taking refuge in the Triple Gem. When we are sick we should perform rituals and recite Sutras and mantras and so on in addition to taking the prescribed medicine. There are some who say that having taken refuge in the Triple Gem, one must not recite mantras or take medicine, because to do so shows lack of faith and will damage one's refuge precept. However, this is a mistaken notion; Buddha himself taught that we must both take medicine and recite Sutras when we are ill.

(ii) The individual precepts of taking refuge

Having taken refuge in Buddha, we must not regard others, such as mundane gods or higher ordinary beings, as our principal spiritual guides. We should rely solely upon Buddha as the true teacher of the path to liberation. Having taken refuge in the Dharma, we must abandon harming other sentient beings and we must not rely on the teachings of other religions to lead us onto the path to liberation. We must rely on Buddha's teaching as the only path to enlightenment and the ultimate result. Once we take refuge in the Sangha, we must not rely on teachers of other religions and we must not keep those who belong to other faiths as 'spiritual friends.'

We may make offerings to others, even to their shrines, but we must not take refuge in other religious traditions; in fact to do so would impair our refuge vows. Similarly, although we may associate with other religious practitioners as our ordinary worldly friends, we must not keep them as spiritual friends. If we do so, it will harm our refuge vows. Similarly, we may make offerings or even prostrate to powerful worldly gods such as Brahma and Indra or even to powerful local people and spirits, but we must never take refuge in them, because this would impair our vow of taking refuge in Buddha.

Some people say that not respecting the scriptures, for example by walking over Dharma texts or by selling them, is a great fault and that this will impair our commitment of taking refuge in the Dharma. This is incorrect. Although showing such disrespect to the scriptures is definitely a fault, it nevertheless does not constitute impairing our refuge vow. There are some people who say there is no need to study and understand Buddha's teachings. However, not studying the scriptures is a far greater impairment to our affirmation in Dharma, because if we do not study the Doctrine, there is no way we will be able to engage successfully in the practices leading to realization. If there are no individuals who have attained realization, there will be no one to explain the scriptural teachings correctly, and the Dharma will eventually degenerate. Therefore obstructing the study and teaching of the Dharma is a far, far greater fault than showing disrespect towards Dharma texts.

With regard to the precept of taking refuge in the Sangha, some claim that if we do not respect symbols such as the clothes they wear, we impair our vow of taking refuge in the Sangha. This is incorrect. Although failure to show respect to Dharma robes is no doubt a fault, it is a far greater fault to show disrespect to fully ordained persons themselves, or to those who teach and practise the Dharma. To do so really would impair our refuge in the Sangha.

(4) The benefits of taking refuge

A temporary benefit of taking refuge in the Triple Gem is being able to dispel the various obscurations, to overcome or at least reduce the sufferings of body and mind, and to avoid being harmed by other people or even by harmful spirits. There is a story which illustrates how neither other people nor spirits can harm one who has taken refuge. At one time, there was a very old man who became a monk, although he possessed no knowledge of the Doctrine. One day a woman made him an offering of a beautiful piece of cloth with a request for him to give Dharma teachings to her. The old monk was very embarrassed, because he did not know any Dharma. However, because he had accepted the cloth, he had to say something. Thinking out loud, he said, 'It is because of my ignorance that I am suffering.' The woman interpreted what he had said as: 'Due to the cause of ignorance, all sufferings arise in the world.' She reflected carefully on the monk's words and concluded that what he had said was very wise. Through meditating further on these words, she acquired understanding of the truth of suffering, the first of the four noble truths, and achieved a great result.

This piece of cloth soon became quite famous. At one point a thief heard about it and decided to steal it. He went to the monk's house and stood at the door, asking for the cloth. The old monk was afraid to go out, so he instructed the thief that if he wanted the piece of cloth, he should go to the side window. So the thief went to the side window, stuck his hand through it and said, 'Now give me that cloth.' The old monk replied, 'When this piece of cloth was given to me, it was given with two hands. So if you want to take it, you should put both hands through the window, and then I will give it to you.' When the thief put both his hands through the window, the monk caught hold of them, bound them with a rope and tied them to a pillar inside the house. Then he went outside, picked up a stick and started beating the thief very hard, one stroke for each line of the refuge formula: 'I take refuge in the Buddha, I take refuge in the Dharma, I take refuge in the Sangha.' When he stopped, the thief's legs were badly hurt and he was in great pain. Then the old monk let him loose and the thief ran away, limping from the pain of his beating. Someone saw him running and asked him why he was limping. The thief replied that he had been trying to steal a piece of cloth from an old monk who caught him and beat him up, and while beating him the old monk had recited the refuge formula. He said that Buddha must be very great indeed, because he had managed to condense the entire refuge prayer into three lines. Otherwise, he would surely have been dead by now!

This thief lived under a bridge which many spirits used to cross every night. One night when these spirits arrived at the bridge, they found they could not get over; there was a strong force holding them back. Curious to find out what was happening, they began to search around. After a while they discovered the thief under the bridge, mumbling to himself. He told them he was reciting the prayer of taking refuge in the Triple Gem. These spirits decided that since this Triple Gem was powerful enough to prevent them from crossing the bridge, they would take refuge also. It is said that these spirits were later reborn in the higher realms. As to the thief, his faith in the Triple Gem was reconfirmed, and later he took full ordination.

Through taking refuge, not only do we overcome harm, we also gain many positive qualities. For example, when we become Buddhist, we attain the qualities of being Buddhist. Our lives become holy and purposeful. By taking the proper refuge and becoming holy people, we become worthy to receive offerings from gods and humans who appreciate Dharma. We will receive protection wherever we are. We will always have the Triple Gem with us as we pass through life, and be content and confident in any situation which arises. We will not be separated from the Triple Gem in this life or in future lifetimes. These are the temporary benefits of taking refuge.

As to the ultimate benefits of taking refuge, by taking refuge in Buddha, we will be able to gain Buddhahood ourselves; by taking refuge in the Dharma, we will be able to teach the Dharma to others; and by taking refuge in the Sangha, we will have many beings gathering to receive teachings from us when we attain Buddhahood. Both those who come to us for teachings and those we seek out in order to teach will benefit, because our teachings will help them gain the stage of full and perfect enlightenment.

With regard to the etymological meaning, the Sanskrit words *saranam gacchami* mean 'I go for refuge.' It is 'refuge' because it protects. One goes, because one approaches in order to take refuge.

3

Generating the
Great Enlightenment Thought

This is the third of the ten stages of practice expounded in the
Mahayanasutralamkara. Broadly speaking, the enlightenment
thought refers to an intention to attain enlightenment. This is similar
to what happens when we decide to embark on a journey; we must
have the intention to take a trip before we actually embark on it.

Each of the four Indian philosophical schools has its own set of
teachings on the enlightenment thought. The concept of producing
the intention to attain enlightenment is present among both
Hinayana and Mahayana practitioners. The Hinayana school
distinguishes three types of enlightenment thought:

(1) the intention of gaining the state of shravaka arhat is a
    Shravakayana enlightenment thought;
(2) the intention of gaining the state of pratyekabuddha is a
    Pratyekabuddhayana enlightenment thought; and
(3) the intention of gaining the state of full and perfect
    enlightenment is the thought of fully enlightened
    Buddhahood.

The Hinayana (Shravakayana and Pratyekabuddhayana)
enlightenment thought, referred to as 'small enlightenment thought,'
is directed to one's own benefit alone. The Mahayana enlightenment
thought is the intention to work for the benefit of others; therefore it
is called the 'great enlightenment thought.' Within the Mahayana

school, there are two systems for generating the great enlightenment thought. One is that of the Mind-Only or Cittamatrin school and the other is that of the Middle Way or Madhyamika school. The Mind-Only school's system of generating the enlightenment thought originated with the great Bodhisattva Maitreya and was transmitted to the Indian saint Asanga and others, such as Chandragomin. It was passed down through these great masters and eventually arrived in Tibet, where it was practised by the early Kadampa school, and later on by the Gelug school. The system advocated by the Madhyamika school originated with Bodhisattva Manjushri and was passed down to Nagarjuna and to other great scholars and saints, such as Shantideva. When it came to Tibet, it was practised by other Tibetan Buddhist schools. The differences between these two systems of generating the great enlightenment thought relate to matters such as the qualities of the teacher who bestows the bodhisattva vows, the characteristics of the one who receives them, the precepts to be followed and the methods for restoring them if they are broken. According to certain teachers, even some within Sakya, these differences are substantial. According to other scholars, however, there is no significant difference between the respective systems of these two schools.

There are two stages to the great enlightenment thought: the aspiring enlightenment thought and the engaging enlightenment thought. The aspiring enlightenment thought is the aspiration to gain the state of full and complete enlightenment for the sake of all sentient beings. In other words, it is the resolve to attain the result of complete Buddhahood. The engaging enlightenment thought is the resolve to engage in the causes to produce that result. It consists of various methods of practising the accumulations of merit and wisdom in order to accomplish the objective of the aspiring enlightenment thought.

The great enlightenment thought may also be categorized into relative enlightenment thought and ultimate enlightenment thought. According to most early Tibetan scholars, both the aspiring enlightenment thought and the engaging enlightenment thought come under the category of relative enlightenment thought. The term 'ultimate enlightenment thought' refers to the transcendental wisdom directly realizing the real nature of phenomena as ultimately devoid of all characteristics and free from all conceptualizations. According to certain teachers, both the relative and the ultimate enlightenment thoughts can be generated through rituals. However, Sakya Pandita strongly refutes this proposition. He maintains that only the relative enlightenment thought can be taken through a ritual, whereas the ultimate enlightenment thought can arise only through meditation. This is because it is the actual uncommon realization of ultimate reality, which is attained only from the first bhumi onwards.

According to the teachings of Bodhisattva Maitreya, there are five ways to produce the relative enlightenment thought:

- through a spiritual friend who explains what the enlightenment thought is and what its benefits are;
- by awakening one's race and thereby creating the cause for entering into the enlightenment thought;
- by accumulating great amounts of merit;
- by studying and listening to the teachings, whereby one learns of the benefits of the enlightenment thought, the qualities of Buddha and the profound teachings of the Mahayana; and
- by continuously habituating the mind to perform virtuous deeds.

There are four traditions for bestowing the Mahayana enlightenment thought:

- the Mind-Only school method, which is explained in great detail in the work *Twenty Verses Concerning the Enlightenment Thought*, by Acharya Chandragomin;
- the method practised by the Madhyamika school, which is explained below;
- the tradition arising from the great mahasiddhas, given during the Sakya Lamdre teachings, which originated with Birwapa (Virupa) and Naropa; and
- the vows of the enlightenment thought taken during Tantric initiation. When one recites the Vajrayana Sevenfold Prayer, one receives the bodhisattva vows (which are the vows of the enlightenment thought).

The enlightenment thought according to the Madhyamika school

The Madhyamika school divides the rituals for bestowing the enlightenment thought into two sections: one consists of the rituals relating to the aspiring enlightenment thought and the other of the rituals relating to the engaging enlightenment thought.

The precepts of the aspiring enlightenment thought

The precepts relating to the aspiring enlightenment thought may be practised in any one of three forms: brief, middle length or extensive.

(1) Brief precepts

The brief form of the aspiring enlightenment thought vow is the wish 'I must attain the state of full and perfect enlightenment for the sake of all sentient beings,' taken with the intention never to discard this wish. This represents all the precepts of producing the enlightenment thought.

(2) Middle-length precepts

When we take the vow of the enlightenment thought, we might find ourselves despairing of ever being able to actualize the wish to gain the state of full and perfect enlightenment for the sake of all sentient beings. If that thought arises, we must overcome it. The intention of overcoming this thought is the middle length practice of the aspiring enlightenment thought. It is divided into three parts:

(i)   overcoming discouragement at the beginning;
(ii)   overcoming discouragement later; and
(iii) overcoming the wish to abandon the enlightenment thought through fear of worldly existence.

(i) Overcoming discouragement at the beginning

We may have doubts about whether or not we have sufficient strength, power and courage and thereby fail to create the resolve to persevere. We may think that the difference between us and the Buddha, who has such excellent qualities and such high realization, is so vast that we could never aspire to such a state. As a result of such thoughts, we may even decide to abandon the enlightenment thought altogether. The whole purpose of the middle form of the vow is to help us realize that such ideas are obstructing our enlightenment thought, and to provide us with methods to overcome them. With regard to this, Maitreya pointed out that since at every moment there is someone somewhere in the world attaining enlightenment, there is no reason why we cannot do so also. The great Bodhisattva Shantideva stated that not only ordinary people but even insects and bugs have the ability to gain liberation and omniscience, provided they possess enough enthusiasm. If even they have this possibility, so much more so do we. Since we have attained the precious human rebirth, we have the power to understand what conduct to engage in and what to refrain from. In this way, by calling such thoughts to mind, we can overcome discouragement.

There is a story showing that a great result may arise from even the tiniest of causes. It is said that at one time there were seven worms sitting on a leaf. This leaf was blown into a stream, which then carried it to the ocean. Owing to the prevailing wind and the current, the leaf eventually circled three times around an image of Vairochana, which was sitting at the bottom of the ocean. Even though these worms had lacked the motivation to circumambulate the image, they were nevertheless reborn in the next life as seven women, due to the merit arising from that circumambulation. Although the seven worms were reborn as poor women belonging to a very low caste, they were able to cut grass and to collect wood and sell it. With what they earned from these menial tasks, they made many offerings and accumulated many virtuous deeds. In consequence, they were reborn in a future life, at the time of Buddha Kashyapa, as seven daughters of a king named King Krikin. During that lifetime, they made many offerings to Buddha Kashyapa, who explained to them how they had come to be born as daughters of the king. He also predicted that the seven sisters would eventually gain the state of full and perfect enlightenment. So from a tiny cause, which arose even without the proper motivation, these seven worms were eventually able to gain the state of perfect enlightenment.

There is another story dating from the time of Buddha Shakyamuni. According to this story, a layman decided to become a monk, so he went to see Shariputra to request full ordination. Shariputra used his clairvoyance to look into the man's past but could not see any cause for giving him ordination. He therefore told the man that since he had never performed any appropriate virtuous deeds, it would not be right to ordain him at that time. The layman was upset by this response, so he went to Buddha and told him what had happened. Buddha replied that it was not correct to say he had not performed any appropriate virtuous deeds at all. In fact, a very long time previously, that man had been born as a pig. One day as this pig was being chased by a dog, it ran around a stupa three times. The merit accrued from this act was sufficient cause for his ordination. Buddha himself then bestowed ordination on that man, and it is said that he gained shravaka arhatship in that very lifetime. Although Shariputra certainly had clairvoyance and could understand other peoples' minds, he was only an arhat. Thus his powers were limited with regard to time and space, and he could not see all the deeds performed by others.

There is another story about a woman who made an offering of rice to Buddha. Buddha predicted that as a result of making this offering, she would gain fortunate rebirths in the realms of gods and men for many lifetimes and that eventually she would attain the state of pratyekabuddha. She related this to her husband, who replied that it was absurd for Buddha to tell such a lie just for the sake of a bowl of rice. He went to see Buddha and asked him why he needed to lie in that way. Buddha was just making trouble for himself by telling such an enormous falsehood merely for the sake of a tiny bowl of rice, he said. Buddha responded by asking him the size of the seed that had produced the nyagrodha tree in the man's back yard. The man replied that the seed had actually been very small, even smaller than a mustard seed. Buddha then pointed out that the husband could see, from the example of this tree, how a very small cause could produce a vast result. The man was convinced by what Buddha said, and went on to gain the first bhumi in that very lifetime.

There were similar cases of people who, merely by offering a small sprig of herb to Buddha, produced the enlightenment thought and were able to gain the state of enlightenment. There were others who gave a very small length of cloth or just a little drinking water. Even from such small causes, they were able to produce the enlightenment thought and gain the result. There is therefore no reason why we should be discouraged about ever being able to gain enlightenment.

If we do not produce the altruistic enlightenment thought and instead endeavour to attain the liberation of the Hinayana, our attainment of complete Buddhahood will be considerably delayed. Since this is the case, we should produce the great enlightenment thought and begin to engage constantly in the Mahayana practices without further delay. This is because the suffering engendered by remaining in worldly existence will be much greater than the difficulties we will encounter while following the spiritual path.

(ii) Overcoming discouragement later

When we perform acts of generosity, we may perhaps expect to gain the result immediately and get rich quickly. However, instead we may be reduced to poverty and thus become discouraged. It could be that because we do not receive the blessings of the deity all at once, we lose heart and decide to abandon our sadhana practice. Similarly, we may become discouraged if our efforts to help a sick friend or relative fail. If the person dies despite many rituals and other Dharma practices, we may decide to abandon the practices completely. However, we should realize that if someone is very sick and dies, even after rituals have been performed, it may be due to the exhaustion of any of the seven causes which maintain life. If none of these is restored, the person will die. There are three main causes of death:

- exhaustion of life force;
- exhaustion of karma from previous lives; and
- exhaustion of merits.

Any one of these alone may act as the cause of death. Furthermore, death may be caused by a combination of any two or three of these factors operating together. Thus from these three main causes, there are in all seven causes of death. If the life force is exhausted, one should restore it by carrying out certain rituals or meditations on long-life deities, such as Amitayus or Ushnisha Vijaya. If previous bad deeds are the cause of impending death, one should release animals in danger of being killed or dying accidentally. This will purify karma. If a person's merit is exhausted, it can be restored by various means, such as making offerings to buddhas and bodhisattvas, reciting scriptures such as Sutras, making offerings to the Sangha, practising generosity to those in need and making food offerings to worldly spirits. One may also substitute nonvirtue with virtue through creating virtuous thoughts and in other ways counteracting nonvirtuous thoughts if they arise in the mind. These are some of the methods for prolonging life.

If only one of these three (life force, karma or merit) is exhausted, there are remedies for prolonging a person's life. If any two are exhausted, then although it is more difficult, it is still possible to avert death. However, if all three are exhausted simultaneously, not even Buddha can prevent death. Therefore if someone dies even after all such rituals have been performed, it shows that all three have been exhausted simultaneously.

We should understand that there are three types of karma:

- the first, strongest karma, which produces results in the present lifetime;
- the second, less powerful karma, which produces results in the next lifetime; and
- the third, weaker karma, which produces results from the third lifetime onwards.

For a result to arise in this lifetime, the deed must be extremely powerful. Such a deed, whether virtuous or nonvirtuous, also requires that the recipient be most extraordinary, such as a fully enlightened being, an arya or one's parents in the present life; the motivation must be absolutely overwhelming; and the article employed in executing the deed must be exceedingly potent. Thus it is very unusual for a result to arise within one lifetime.

Sometimes we may notice that a person who has performed many virtuous deeds in this life appears to experience a lot of suffering, while someone who has committed a lot of nonvirtue seems to experience lots of happiness. Some may even think that suffering specifically singles out followers of the Buddha's path. However, we should understand that such experiences of suffering and happiness are the results of deeds committed in previous lives, not during this lifetime. Everyone suffers until he or she attains the state of enlightenment. It is said that even shravaka arhats have to suffer. For example, Maudgalaputra was murdered, and another arhat died after eating grass ashes. The practice of Dharma does not preclude one from experiencing suffering. Nevertheless, the final outcome of practising Dharma is to eliminate all our suffering completely.

Some new practitioners may think that by making a few offerings one day they will have good dreams that night or that something wonderful will happen to them right away. Some people practise sadhana for one or two days with the expectation that they will meet one of the deities the very next day. They may even think that one of the buddhas will walk into their room, shake their hand and congratulate them on the quality of their meditation. But the results cannot arise so quickly from practising only a small amount of virtue. When we first begin to practise, we simply have not created sufficient causes or conditions for the results to arise.

The reason why the results of a practice cannot arise immediately is that the result arises only from the complete assembly of all its causes and conditions. The result simply cannot arise unless all the causes and conditions converge. For example, if we plant a flower seed and expect to see the flower appear within that same day or the next, we will be disappointed. Similarly, if we are ill and expect to recover immediately by performing a small act of virtue, this will not happen, because all the causes and conditions will not yet be in place. Furthermore, if the result were to arise at an improper time, when all the causes and conditions had not yet come together, it would disprove the law of cause and effect. This is because it would show that it is possible for the result to arise before its causes are complete.

In addition, it would be unwise to expect the results of virtuous actions to ripen quickly, because then we would have to accept that the results of nonvirtue would also ripen quickly. If the results of nonvirtue appeared immediately, we would experience constant suffering, because we commit a lot of nonvirtue every day, through our deeds of body, speech and mind. Similarly, if we performed a small amount of virtue and gained a very rapid result, the happiness would disappear almost immediately. So it is actually better for the result not to ripen until the proper time, when all its particular causes and conditions are assembled.

(iii) Overcoming the wish to abandon the enlightenment thought through fear of worldly existence

Some Mahayana followers may give up their enlightenment thought altogether, for fear of having to experience great hardships. They may not believe they will be able to respond peacefully when someone harms them and might think that they may consequently be stuck in the sufferings of cyclic existence for a very long time. However, if a person harms us, we should understand that by harming him in return we only create further suffering. Therefore whenever we experience harm, we should respond with compassion and loving-kindness. In this way we are able to neutralize any harm done to us. We must meditate on this.

We should call to mind that this world (including the outer world, its inhabitants and our inner experiences) is by its very nature unreal; it has no existence of its own; it is like a magician's creations. If we understand this, we can overcome fear of worldly suffering.

Some may think it takes too long to reach enlightenment for the benefit of others and not be prepared to stay around for the duration. If we are in danger of losing bodhicitta because of the length of time it takes to practise on the path, we should endeavour to understand what actually constitutes an aeon and what constitutes a moment. We should meditate on this. In this way we will discover that there is ultimately no difference between an aeon and an instant. 'Long' and 'short' are just conceptualisations, lacking inherent existence. In ultimate reality, time does not even exist.

Yet another way to overcome the wish to give up the enlightenment thought is through praying to the buddhas, to the great bodhisattvas or to personal deities. In short, through techniques such as these, we can overcome any inclination to relinquish the enlightenment thought.

(3) The extensive precepts

There are three parts to the extensive way of practising the precepts of the enlightenment thought.

    (i)   the cause of generating the enlightenment thought;

    (ii) the methods to enhance our enlightenment thought; and

    (iii) the methods to avoid impairing our enlightenment thought.

(i) The cause of generating the enlightenment thought
The cause of generating the enlightenment thought is to arouse thoughts of loving-kindness and great compassion.

(ii) The methods to enhance our enlightenment thought .
There are seven circumstances which cause the aspiring enlightenment thought to grow:

(1) to take a true spiritual friend as one's teacher;

(2) to produce aspiring and trusting faith in the Triple Gem;

(3) to recognize and avoid the obstructing deeds of Mara;

(4) to pray to the buddhas and bodhisattvas in the ten directions that Mara's deeds not be performed;

(5) to cultivate understanding of the benefits of the enlightenment thought and the faults of both samsara and nirvana;

(6) to call to mind the great qualities of the buddhas and bodhisattvas, such as their miraculous powers and supramundane knowledge; and

(7) to generate joyful enthusiasm in accomplishing the well-being of self and others.

If we have cultivated these seven, we will understand the faults of cyclic existence and develop the intention not to commit evil deeds. Seeing the faults of nirvana, we will avoid developing great desire for emptiness. Seeing the great benefits of the enlightenment thought both for ourselves and others, we won't despair of cyclic existence. Seeing the excellent qualities of the buddhas and bodhisattvas, we will rejoice in the temporary and ultimate results of spiritual practice. We can prevent the evil deeds of Mara from arising by making supplications to the preceptor and the Triple Gem, and by doing so we will be sustained by the power of the buddhas and bodhisattvas. In this way, we can augment our thought of awakening by removing opposing forces and enhancing favourable conditions.

(iii) The methods to avoid impairing our enlightenment thought

- To overcome losing faith in the Guru and the Triple Gem, we should instil within ourselves proper faith in the buddhas and in the Guru. In this way we will obstruct improper thoughts such as anger from arising.
- To overcome being jealous about the prosperity of others, we should generate thoughts of great joy about their prosperity and be pleased they have attained what we wished for them.
- To overcome thinking of benefiting ourselves alone, we should meditate on cherishing others instead.
- To overcome reluctance towards practising the skilful means of the perfections and contenting ourselves with merely recognizing the nature of the mind, we need to reflect upon the qualities of the path and the result.
- To overcome our ignorance concerning the qualities of the enlightened ones and our consequent lack of motivation to emulate them, we must carefully study the qualities of the buddhas and bodhisattvas. Having understood their qualities, we must embark on the various practical means of attaining these qualities ourselves.

The precepts of the engaging enlightenment thought

So far we have discussed the three sets of training for the aspiring enlightenment thought. There are also three sets of training pertaining to the engaging enlightenment thought: the brief, the middle-length and the extensive.

(1) Brief precepts

We should refrain from committing nonvirtuous deeds and perform as many virtuous deeds as possible. If it happens that we commit a nonvirtuous deed in the morning, through heedlessness or powerful afflictive emotions, we must confess it that night. Similarly, any nonvirtue committed during the night must be confessed the following morning. The merit accrued from our virtuous deeds must always be dedicated to gaining full and perfect enlightenment in order to liberate all sentient beings.

(2) Middle-length precepts

With regard to the middle-length precepts of the engaging enlightenment thought, these involve discarding the four black dharmas and adopting the four white dharmas. This is because committing the four black dharmas will lead the practitioner to forget the enlightenment thought during the next life, whereas adopting the four white dharmas will enable him to develop the manifested enlightenment thought during the next life.

The four black dharmas are:

(i) to deceive the Guru, the Triple Gem or those who are worthy of our veneration;

(ii) to tell those who are practising virtue, especially those practising the Mahayana path, that they are on the wrong path, thereby instilling regret or doubt in their minds;

(iii) to criticize or disparage those who have engaged in the Mahayana path; and

(iv) lacking the altruistic motivation, to deceive or trick sentient beings.

The four white dharmas are:

(i) not to tell lies deliberately;

(ii) to live altruistically with other sentient beings, without deceit or pretence;

(iii) to view all the Bodhisattvas of the Four Directions as the Great Teacher (Buddha) and offer praises to them in the four directions; and

(iv) to guide those beings one has been ripening to adhere perfectly to the unsurpassable enlightenment and not to incline towards the Hinayana path.

(3) Extensive precepts

There are three main parts to the extensive precept for training in the engaging enlightenment thought:

(i) the cause for the engaging enlightenment thought to arise;

(ii) how to cultivate the conditions for expanding the engaging enlightenment thought; and

  (iii) methods for keeping the engaging enlightenment thought from declining.

(i) The cause for the engaging enlightenment thought to arise

After instilling the aspiring enlightenment thought in our mind, we should use skilful means to develop it and discard any conditions which may tend to weaken it. We must reflect again and again on the sufferings of samsara and the faults of the lower vehicle's liberation.

(ii) How to cultivate the conditions conducive to expanding the engaging enlightenment thought

To create the conditions for augmenting the enlightenment thought, we should recite any seven-limb prayers we know three times by day and three times at night. Additionally, we should also engage in the various deeds performed by buddhas and bodhisattvas, such as generosity and so on and other virtuous deeds. Examples of such deeds may be found in the Jatakas.

(iii) Methods for keeping the engaging enlightenment thought from declining

According to the *Akashagarbha Sutra*, the method for not impairing the engaging enlightenment thought is to avoid the root downfalls of the bodhisattva vows. If one breaks any one of them, one should confess it prior to the next session. As mentioned earlier, one method to avoid weakening our bodhisattva vows is to rely on our yidam or personal deity. To illustrate this, there is a story about a great Indian teacher by the name of Dignaga who was successful in maintaining his enlightenment thought through relying on Manjushri.

  Dignaga was born as the son of a very rich and powerful king in the south of India. When he grew up, he renounced the princely life and entered a Buddhist order. This order followed one of the Hinayana traditions which maintained the view of a truly existent self. Now Dignaga had heard that the concept of a real self was not accepted in Buddhism. Nevertheless, as this was the view held by the abbot of his monastery, he was reluctant to contradict him. In case he himself might be mistaken, he decided to give this theory of the existence of a personal self the benefit of the doubt. So he began to carry out some investigations. In order to see better during the day, he opened four new windows in his room and burned four lamps at night. Then he undertook a meticulous and protracted examination of his body to see whether he could locate this self his abbot taught about. At times he would even remove all his clothes and stand naked in front of a mirror. However, search as he might, he could not locate the self.

Some of the monks in the monastery noticed his strange behaviour and reported it to the abbot. So the abbot sent for Dignaga and told him that since he had renounced the world, he should behave properly and stop acting strangely in his room. Dignaga told the abbot that he had been trying to find the self the abbot had spoken about, and thought that his impure vision might have been obstructing him from seeing it. Afterwards, he made four new windows and burned even more lamps, in an effort to find this self. Since he was still unable to find it, he informed his abbot that the view of the existence of a self must be incorrect. The abbot replied, 'All the other monks in the monastery have accepted this view of the self, yet you have denied it and developed a negative, nihilistic view. That being the case, it would be better for you to leave.'

After this, Dignaga decided to go up into the mountains and meditate. On the way he met another prince, who noticed the sign of a wheel on Dignaga's foot. He told him that if he were to become a king, he would be very powerful. He was willing to give half of his kingdom to Dignaga if he would agree to join him. But Dignaga told him that he could see no point in ruling a kingdom within worldly existence or wielding worldly power. Instead, Dignaga found a cave, where he embarked on studying and meditating on the teachings of Lord Buddha.

During his study, he realized that one would have to consult a great number of texts in order to learn the meanings of Buddha's words. He decided to collect all these teachings together into a condensed format. First he wrote some small texts containing Buddhist logic. Then he decided to produce a comprehensive logic text. He first wrote a message telling Buddha of his intention and placed this message on the wall of his cave. As he did this, many wonderful signs such as earthquakes appeared, and the entire area was bathed in light.

A Hindu Mimamsaka scholar and meditator perceived these signs. Through his clairvoyant powers, he learned that Dignaga was going to write a substantial textbook on logic and realized that if he did so, it might harm the tirthikas (non-Buddhist philosophical schools). So whenever Dignaga left on his alms round, the Mimamsaka scholar would use his powers to erase the passages Dignaga wrote. Every time he did this, Dignaga would rewrite the verse. This occurred three times. On the fourth day, Dignaga left a message inviting the person who had been erasing his verses to meet him and explain his reasons for doing so.

That day, the Mimamsaka scholar waited for him, and when Dignaga returned to the cave, the two debated about the correct view of ultimate reality. Dignaga won the debate, and according to the custom of the time, he insisted that the Hindu scholar renounce his religion immediately and convert to Buddhism. The scholar refused. Instead, he used his supernatural powers to emit an enormous flame from his mouth, which singed Dignaga's hair and beard. Though the fire was so powerful that it consumed even the trees around the outside of the cave, it could not harm Dignaga, because he had produced the enlightenment thought. After this, the Hindu scholar flew away.

Later Dignaga reflected that in return for all his work for the Dharma, his hair and beard had been singed, and despite his good motivation for debating, he had been unable to convert even a single person. Therefore how could there be any point in trying to gain Buddhahood for the sake of all sentient beings? Thinking in this vein, he wrote a message on a piece of wood stating his intention to give up the enlightenment thought, and tossed the piece of wood high into the air. He resolved that from the very moment the wood landed, he would give up his enlightenment thought and never work for the sake of sentient beings again. But the piece of wood did not land. When Dignaga looked up into the sky to see what had happened, he saw Manjushri holding it. He asked Manjushri why he had taken hold of it. Manjushri replied by inquiring what he was doing, and Dignaga explained what had happened. Manjushri then requested Dignaga not to give up his enlightenment thought. He promised to stay with him and act as his spiritual guide until Dignaga had attained the first bhumi. He said that Dignaga's philosophical writings were extremely valuable and that he should continue his work, because it would benefit many sentient beings.

4

The Perfection of Generosity

The fourth of the ten stages of practice expounded in the *Mahayanasutralamkara* is 'accomplishing the perfections of generosity and the remaining perfections.' The word 'perfection' is a translation of the Sanskrit word *paramita*, which literally means 'has reached the far shore.' Here it signifies having transcended or gone beyond both worldly existence and personal liberation. The practice of the six paramitas, or perfections, constitutes the sole method for accomplishing the principal objective of the enlightenment thought. The first of the six perfections is the perfection of generosity.

The act of generosity means giving away one's inner and outer possessions to others with the intention of benefiting them. The mind wishing to give is the principal thought underlying the act of generosity. If the act of generosity is motivated by the enlightenment thought (the wish to attain enlightenment for the sake of all sentient beings) and conjoined with an understanding of the emptiness of the three factors (the giver, the recipient and the article)—which is the proper view of ultimate reality—and provided that the merits are dedicated at the conclusion to the benefit of all sentient beings, it becomes the perfection of generosity.

There are three unfavourable conditions which may obstruct us from engaging in the perfection of generosity:

(1) miserliness;
(2) impure generosity; and
(3) lack of the enlightenment thought.

(1) Miserliness

With regard to the fault of miserliness, we should be aware that although using our possessions may bring us some happiness during this lifetime, giving our things away to others will be a source of happiness to others in this life and to ourselves in future lifetimes. However, if instead of using our possessions for our own benefit or giving them away to others, we just hold onto them through miserliness, this will produce nothing but suffering, both in this life and in future lifetimes.

Miserliness leads only to suffering. There is absolutely no benefit in it. Sakya Pandita explains that if we give away our property in this life, it is just like putting it into a secure bank; we will be provided with whatever we need in future lives. In other words, there is great benefit in being generous, because the result will be available to be used at some time in the future. On the other hand, if we are miserly, we will never be able to use our things. Somebody else will eventually take them and make use of them. We will be just like bees, which work so hard to gather honey, only to have it removed by someone else. If we are miserly in this life, the result will be rebirth in the realm of the hungry ghosts. And then even if we do gain a human rebirth after coming out of the hungry ghost realm, we will experience dire poverty.

(2) Impure generosity

If we give impurely, there will be no benefit either in this lifetime or in the future, only suffering. For example, if we plant a seed in salty earth, it will be impossible for the seed to ripen, and for the plant to grow and bear fruit. It is akin to giving dead fish to a bird which is only able to consume live fish. Instead of helping, it will harm the bird.

(3) Lack of the enlightenment thought

Even if we engage in giving pure gifts, our giving will not be a cause for gaining Buddhahood unless we produce the enlightenment thought. Although we may gain certain benefits through giving even if we do not produce the enlightenment thought, the result will be experienced only once and then will be exhausted, never to increase. One may gain wealth in a future rebirth, for instance, but this benefit will be only of short duration. Similarly, as long as we aim only for our own personal liberation, even if we dedicate the merit, the merit will soon be exhausted and will not increase.

Next we will examine the remedy for overcoming unfavourable conditions to practising the perfection of generosity. When we look at the antidote for miserliness, we should realize that miserliness is just a product of our desirous attachment. That being the case, desirous attachment must be overcome. To do so, we should first come to an understanding of its disadvantages and of how it causes us to suffer. First we suffer through struggling to collect the things we want; once we obtain them, we worry about protecting them from theft or destruction by others; and when they are finally destroyed or stolen, we experience the suffering of their loss. So desirous attachment causes suffering at every stage of our involvement with possessions, from the time of trying to acquire them, to the time of trying to keep them, right up to the time of losing them. There is therefore absolutely no point in being attached to possessions.

Sakya Pandita says that when we lack possessions, we go through the suffering of wanting to acquire them. When we have a few articles, we go through the suffering of not being satisfied with what we have and of wanting more. When we have many possessions, we still have the suffering of not being satisfied. When we lose our possessions, we have the suffering of being deprived of them. Furthermore, when the defilement of desirous attachment is present, our mind manifests many other afflictive emotions such as jealousy, anger, miserliness, deceit and so on. When these arise, we may be inclined to perform impure deeds such as lying, stealing or killing even our own kind parents. Therefore, as it is clear from many points of view that desirous attachment causes immense suffering, we should try first to weaken the manifested desirous attachment and then uproot it completely.

There is a story to illustrate the unfavourable consequences of not being satisfied with our possessions. There was once a king who became extremely powerful after inheriting his father's kingdom. He was known as a universal emperor because he had acquired all the signs, such as a thousand children, a thousand wheels and a thousand elephants, and he had vast power over many men. In his kingdom there were five hundred meditators belonging to a heretical sect. One day while meditating, they were disturbed by the noise of birds flying overhead. Thereupon they made a wish that the wings of all the birds would become diseased and they would lose the ability to fly. As a consequence of that wish, all those birds lost the power of flight and had to walk on the ground from then on. When the king saw this, he enquired how it had happened. He was told that this was the work of the meditators. The king decided he would not allow people with such evil thoughts to stay within the bounds of his kingdom. Accordingly, he issued a proclamation banishing all five hundred meditators. Since the king was so powerful and his kingdom was so vast that it spanned the four continents, the meditators had nowhere to go, except to the slopes of Mount Sumeru.

Now this king possessed such merit that whatever he wished for would materialize. At one time, seeing that there would be great prosperity in the land if everyone had plenty of grain to eat, the king prayed, 'May grain fall from the sky.' Thereupon a great rain of grain of all kinds fell from the sky. Naturally, the people became curious to know whose merit had caused this. They wondered whether it had happened due to their own merit or to that of the king. So they asked the king on several occasions. Finally the king made the wish, 'May a great rain of jewels fall onto the grounds of the palace and may only coins fall outside it.' The king told the people it had been a great mistake on their part to think that the rain of grain resulted from their merit. It was because of their improper thinking that the jewels had fallen only into the palace; otherwise the jewels would have fallen throughout the kingdom. In any case, he gave the jewels away.

From time to time, this king would ask his subjects whether there were any parts of the world not under his control. Whenever they told him about such places, he went out and conquered them. He also went to the ocean, where there were great kingdoms of naga spirits, and he conquered them, too. He ventured as far as Mount Sumeru, where naga spirits were living along with various lower heavenly deities. Because they put up such strong resistance, the king made a wish that whoever fought him would have to run away. So vast was his merit that everyone who fought against him did indeed run away. Thus he was able to conquer all the lower parts of Mount Sumeru as far as the lower heavens. Finally he arrived at the Heaven of the Thirty-Three, the abode of the great heavenly king Shakra. Thereupon Shakra bestowed half his throne upon the king.

Meanwhile, the five hundred meditators did not believe the king would ever succeed in conquering their dwelling place. When they saw him arriving with his army, one of the most powerful meditators took some water and sprinkled it around to prevent the army from passing beyond that point. Once the king found out that one of the meditators was impeding his army's advance, he asked the meditators to tell him their greatest desire. When they told him they wanted to have long hair, he made a wish for them all to become completely bald and also for them to be driven away. As a result, all the meditators' hair began to fall out and the people were able to chase them away. However, the king's wife remarked that it was not proper to treat them that way, since these were religious practitioners and should not cause trouble to others. So the king simply sent the meditators to another place.

The king remained with Shakra and became extremely powerful. He reached the point where he thought he could fight and conquer the higher gods in addition to the lower gods or demigods. In fact, he began to think he had become as powerful as Indra himself. This was an extremely wicked idea, and it produced a lot of negative karma. Eventually, all the merit he had accumulated in the past was used up. This caused him to fall from the heavenly realms back to the realm of human beings. After some time, he fell into a deplorable condition and reached the point of dying. People around him asked what they should tell the populace about how such a great king had died. He asked them to tell people that what had happened to him was a consequence of his not being satisfied, despite wielding such great power. That king was the present Buddha in one of his previous lives.

Someone once asked Buddha how he had come to gain that birth as a universal emperor. Buddha replied that it was due to karma performed in an earlier life. At one time, when another Buddha had passed by him, he had thrown five grains of pea seeds in that Buddha's direction. Four of the five seeds had landed in the bowl, and one seed had landed on the rim, where it remained. The four seeds which landed in the begging bowl resulted in his becoming the king of four continents, and the seed which landed on the edge resulted in his gaining half the power over the Heaven of the Thirty-Three.

The immediate antidote to miserliness is generosity. There are four types of generosity we can practise:

(1) giving loving-kindness;
(2) giving fearlessness, by delivering those who are in trouble or afraid from danger and suffering;
(3) giving teachings or explaining the Dharma; and
(4) giving material things.

There are three categories of people who can engage in these four kinds of generosity:

(1) those who renounce the world;
(2) lay practitioners; and
(3) noble bodhisattvas.

(1) Those who renounce the world

Those who have renounced the world, such as monks and nuns who have taken pratimoksha vows, should engage in the first three kinds of generosity: giving loving-kindness and compassion, giving fearlessness and giving teachings on the Dharma. With regard to the fourth kind, giving material things, the renounced person should give only pencils, paper, ink and the like. When Buddha Shakyamuni renounced the world and left his father's palace, he returned his horse to his father instead of giving it away. When he received the offering of milk from Sujata in a golden vessel, he drank the milk and returned the vessel to her. When Sujata offered the vessel to him again, Buddha took it and tossed it into the river.

When the followers of other philosophical schools heard what he had done, they concluded that Buddha had made a great mistake. They maintained that he should have given the horse away, instead of returning it to the king, and instead of throwing the gold vessel into the river, he should have given it to the poor. However, Buddha explained that as he had renounced the world, it was not appropriate for him to give such articles to people. Although there might be some short-term benefit from such giving, in the long term the person who took the article would be reborn in the lower realms. The main practice for one who has renounced the world is to engage in study, contemplation and meditation and not in giving material objects. If renunciates were to change their role and make the act of giving objects their main practice, it would create obstacles for practitioners and also for society at large, such as poverty and famine.

(2) Lay practitioners

A lay practitioner, such as a bodhisattva lay practitioner, should first give away things he finds easy to give. For example, in Arya Shantideva's *Bodhicharyavatara* (Engaging in the Activity of the Bodhisattva), it is said that we should begin practising by giving very simple things, such as a few vegetables or a few grains of rice. In this way we won't feel any sense of loss. Once we are able to do this easily, we should gradually increase the value and the amount of what we give. We should continue increasing our potential to give until we are finally able to give away even our own body. By this time we will not even notice any difference between our body and a vegetable. In other words, we won't feel any sense of loss. However, we should not give our body away until we have gained a proper understanding that we are giving away something of no more value than a vegetable. In one sutra, it says that one should begin by first giving a little water, and after accustoming oneself to giving water, one should gradually increase the scale of giving.

A lay practitioner must never engage in impure giving. We should not give to powerful people, such as kings, or to someone for whom we feel strong desire. Also, from the point of view of the article, we should not give improper objects such as meat, alcohol, poison or weapons. From the viewpoint of motivation, we should not give through improper motivation. Giving through improper motivation means to give something away in expectation of gaining something in return, such as a reward in this life or in future lifetimes. It also includes giving to a person who owes us something, hoping that thereby the person will repay us.

The basis for giving is the mind. We will not be able to give properly unless we have developed the right attitude. If we do not create the wish to give, then when we see a beggar in the street, for example, the first thing we will think is, 'Here comes someone who is after my money.' Instead of giving him something, we will want to chase him away. So in order to create the correct basis for the act of giving, we must develop the correct mental attitude—the wish to give joyfully—by reflecting in the following way. When we see a beggar coming towards us, we should remind ourselves that this is an opportunity for us to perform an act of generosity, enabling us to accumulate more merit and also to gain prosperity in future lifetimes. We should also see the beggar as an emanation of Buddha or a bodhisattva and reflect that by giving to him, we are pleasing all buddhas and bodhisattvas. In these ways we should formulate ideas conducive to feeling joy and happiness in the act of giving.

With regard to the recipients of generosity, there may be certain persons we like giving to and others we don't like giving to. For example, there are some who like to give to their teacher but who do not like to give to Buddha, and some who like to give to Buddha but not to others. Some like to give to those who chant the Sutras but not to the monks who study them. Some like to give to monks and nuns but not to others. To redress this bias, we should increase our offerings to those we like giving to and start giving small articles to others, thus training our minds to give happily to all.

With regard to the time of giving, some of us prefer to make offerings only on special occasions like holy days, such as Buddha's enlightenment day, and don't wish to give on other days. To train ourselves in giving at all times, we should begin by increasing our offerings on days when we like to give, and think about giving on the days when we are not accustomed to making offerings. We can start to increase the length of our period of giving, instead of giving just on a particular occasion. For example, we should increase it by promising to perform the practice of generosity for a few days, then for a month, for a year, for ten years and then for a lifetime. Also, with regard to the object, we should start giving small objects such as a glass of water. After that we can give the glass in addition to the water. We can increase the number of articles up to the point when we attain the first bhumi, at which time we will be able to give away our body. By the way, remember that only those who have gained this stage can give their body away!

(3) Noble bodhisattvas

There are three types of giving: giving, giving much and great giving. 'Giving' includes such acts as giving away one's kingdom. 'Giving much' involves giving away not only one's kingdom but also one's children or spouse. 'Great giving' means not only giving these but also giving one's body away. There are many stories about great bodhisattvas who have performed such acts of giving, and we should read them and study them carefully.

Four positive qualities must be associated with the practice of the perfection of generosity:

(1) all forms of its opposite, miserliness, must be discarded;
(2) it must be associated with the nonconceptual realization of ultimate reality, selflessness of persons and phenomena;
(3) by giving away whatever others want, in conformity with the Doctrine, one must have the ability to fulfil the wishes of others; and
(4) after sentient beings have been gathered through the practice of generosity, they must be ripened by being placed on one of the three yanas, according to their temporary race.

There are seven attachments we must abandon while practising each of the six perfections. With regard to the perfection of generosity, these are:

(1) being attached to possessions;
(2) being attached to postponement, thinking that we do not have to give at this point, that we can give later;
(3) being attached to feeling satisfied with whatever we have given;
(4) being attached to expecting returns in this lifetime;
(5) being attached to gaining a result in future lifetimes;
(6) being attached to miserliness, the opposite of generosity; and
(7) being attached to the distractions. There are two kinds of distraction. The first is the distraction of speculation, which means taking pleasure in the lower vehicle. The second is the distraction of conceptual thought, which means conceptually grasping the three factors of the act of giving: the giver, the recipient and the article.

Benefits of generosity

As to the benefits of generosity, one will gain prosperity, fame and happiness during this lifetime. In future lifetimes, one will attain whatever one desires; one will be able to give to others whatever they desire, and one will not be reborn in an evil land or during times of famine and the like. The ultimate beneficial result of the perfection of generosity is that at the time of attaining Buddhahood, one will be able to gather followers of both mundane and supramundane beings, in quantities as vast as the ocean. Furthermore, one will receive an abundance of offerings resulting from virtuous actions and gain mastery over many meditative absorptions, such as the meditative absorption of sky treasury, which enables us to call forth a rain of riches from the sky. These are the particular benefits one will gain from the practice of generosity.

According to Sakya Pandita, there are four stories to be told to illustrate the perfection of generosity. One is about a prince by the name of Sarvatara, who gave away his two children to an old brahmin; another is about a hare which gave up its life; the third is about a king by the name of Moonrays who gave away his head and the fourth is about a king who cut up his body. I will relate the first of these stories.

Once upon a time there was a king by the name of Sarvamitra who, due to his prayers to one of the gods, produced a son with very special qualities. This prince, named Sarvatara, grew up, married and had two children, a boy and a girl. The prince used to tell people that those who possessed wisdom would always practise generosity, while those without wisdom would never do so. At one time, the prince went to a garden outside the palace. As he approached the gate of the garden, the god Shakra decided to test him by taking the form of a poor beggar. When the prince saw him, he became upset, as he had nothing to give him. So he decided not to go into the garden. When the king asked him why he had returned so quickly and looked so disheartened, the prince replied that what he had seen there had depressed him. He asked the king to grant him permission to give from the king's great treasury to those in need. Then, having attained the kings' permission, he set up offices throughout the kingdom to give things away. Many people would go to these offices to make requests, and they were given whatever they asked for. The news of his generosity spread far and wide, and the prince became extremely famous.

Now King Sarvamitra had a formidable enemy, whom he had faced in many a battle. This enemy had always lost, due to the might of one of the king's elephants, known as 'Seven Auspicious Signs.' This elephant was a most extraordinary animal and always turned the tide of battle in the king's favour. Seeing that the prince was always giving things away, this enemy decided to ask him for the king's elephant. At first the prince decided it would be wrong to give it away, as it belonged to the king, and he would be upset to lose such a special elephant. But then he reflected that he had made a promise to fulfil the wishes of everyone who requested anything from him, and he must fulfil his promise. He therefore gave the elephant away.

When people heard what the prince had done, they became afraid that the king would lose in future battles without the help of this great elephant. The king's ministers held a meeting to discuss what to do. On account of all the trouble the prince had caused, some suggested that they cut off his hands, others suggested that they cut off his feet, while still others suggested that they cut off his head. However, the king judged that none of these punishments would be fair, because the prince had simply been practising generosity, without intending any harm. Another minister suggested that the prince be exiled for twelve years, during which time he might come to repent of his reckless acts of giving. The king agreed to this. He later explained to the prince that he would have to go away, as otherwise he would soon deplete the treasury entirely and impoverish the kingdom.

The prince agreed to the king's wishes and informed his wife that he had been exiled. He told her it would be best for her to stay behind and bring the children up properly. The prince's wife disagreed, saying that she could not bear to be separated from him for twelve years. The prince explained it would be difficult for her if she accompanied him, since he wished to continue his acts of generosity, and she would obstruct him. But as she promised not to be an obstacle to his giving, he agreed to take her with him.

When the prince was on the point of setting out, the king became crestfallen. He even relented at the last moment and said it would be better for the prince to stay. He advised his son to give up just those acts of generosity that had caused all the problems. The prince replied that he had no intention of abandoning his practice of giving. So as there was no way he could stay without continuing to give things away, it would be better for him to leave. Since the prince was so popular, the king, his queens and the ministers presented him with many gifts. Even the ordinary subjects were desolate to hear that the prince was leaving.

As the prince travelled to his place of exile, he met many poor people on the way. He began giving away the gifts given to him, including all the jewellery he possessed. It was not long before he had given everything away. Then he met a farmer who needed horses to help him plough his land, so he also gave away the horses they were riding. He continued his journey by pulling the carriage, while his wife helped by pushing from behind. Later on he met someone who wanted a carriage, and he gave that away, too. As they continued on their journey, they met many more people who needed things. Since they had nothing else left to give, they gave away their own clothes and even their children's clothes, until they had given away all their necessities. Finally they arrived at the place of exile. It was very beautiful, owing to the blessings of the bodhisattvas. The prince and his family built a thatched cottage and lived there, meditating on the bodhisattva path and leading a peaceful life.

Not far from the prince's house, there lived an old and ugly brahmin with a young and beautiful wife. Because of the discrepancies in their ages, they were always quarrelling. One day, when the young woman was at the river fetching water, she met a young man who told her that she was stupid to live with such an old and ugly man. When the young woman returned home, she was even more bad-tempered than usual and began causing further trouble. She told her husband what the young man had said and furthermore insisted that he hire servants to fetch water, as she was not prepared to do this any longer. When the old man explained how difficult it was to find servants, she told him about Prince Sarvatara. She insisted that, as he was renowned for his generosity, her husband should request the prince to give his two children to them to work as servants.

Accordingly, the brahmin went to see the prince and told him he had come a great distance to request his two children to work as servants for his wife. The prince reflected that if he gave his children away, they would be forced to work hard and lead a life of misery. Knowing what they would face, it was going to be extremely difficult to give them up. While he was thinking along these lines, the brahmin asked the prince why he was hesitating so much, since he had promised to give away everything he had. The prince agreed that this was true, so he sent for his children and told them he was giving them away, and that they were to obey this old man from then on. As he was in the process of handing his children over to the elderly brahmin, the earth quaked as a sign of the immensity of his altruistic deed.

At first the children were reluctant to leave before their mother returned. However, they could see that their father had made up his mind and there was nothing anybody could do to change it. Once they were outside with the brahmin, it occurred to them that they would never see their mother again. They began to scream and shout. The old brahmin grew alarmed and asked the prince to tie up the children so he could manage to take them away. So the prince bound up his two children and handed the end of the rope to the old brahmin, who started to beat the boy as he led them both away. Wounds appeared on the boy's body which began to bleed. The prince was aghast and cried at the sight of his son's suffering. However, he honoured his promise and did nothing to prevent his children from leaving. Because he had been able to give his children away despite being so grief-stricken, the greatness of his deed was signalled by another earthquake.

Meanwhile the prince's wife, who was out picking fruit, noticed the earthquakes. Her first thought was that something must be happening to her children. She became so alarmed that one of her legs turned numb with shock. As she struggled to run back home, a god noticed her and decided that it would be wrong for her to obstruct the prince's act of generosity. Thereupon he manifested in the form of a lion and placed himself in the mother's path, forcing her to take a long detour to get back home. By the time she arrived, the children were already far away. She could see how upset the prince was and asked him about her children. The prince told her what had happened. Seeing his wife's distress, he explained to her about impermanence and reminded her that sooner or later we must part with everything. He also reminded her of the promise she had made in front of Buddha Dipankara, that she would always be his wife in every future lifetime and that she would never obstruct his acts of generosity. Upon hearing these words, she renewed her vow not to obstruct her husband's practice of generosity.

Then the god Shakra decided to test the prince by requesting from him his wife. Taking the form of an ugly old brahmin, he went to see the prince with this request. So the prince gave away his wife, with the thought that he had now given away his very last possession. He prayed that this might become a cause for gaining Buddhahood. When Shakra and the prince's wife were outside, Shakra confided to her that he was actually Shakra and not a brahmin. He told her that whatever she wished for would be fulfilled. So the prince's wife requested Shakra to release her two children. Shakra then returned the woman to the prince and instructed him not to give her away to anyone else, as she now belonged to him. Then with his powerful vision, Shakra searched for the children and saw them approaching the brahmin's house, together with the old and ugly brahmin. He altered the brahmin's wife's way of thinking so that when she saw the two children, she complained to the brahmin that they were unsuitable to work as servants. She said they had obviously been badly beaten and anyway, they were too small and lean. She told the brahmin to sell them in the market and use the money to buy a larger servant.

Thereupon the brahmin took the children to a small town to sell them. Shakra went there too, transformed into the appearance of a man. When the brahmin approached him and asked him to buy the children, Shakra told him he was not interested. Furthermore, he told the brahmin that to get the price he was asking, he would need to sell them in a larger town. The brahmin heeded his advice and set off to the largest town in the vicinity, which happened to be in the prince's own kingdom. When the people of the kingdom saw the children, they recognized them as the king's grandchildren and considered snatching them back. However, realizing that the prince must have given them away and that to snatch them back would obstruct his practice of generosity, they instead informed the king that a brahmin was trying to sell his grandchildren. Then the king called for the brahmin and bought the children from him.

The king sent out messengers to ask his son to return home. But the prince, who had been away for only eleven years, replied that he would not return until the twelfth year. When he finally set out on the trip back to his father's kingdom, he met the man to whom he had long ago given the precious elephant. This man now offered to return the elephant to him to use as transport, since the journey to the palace was a long and arduous one. Moreover, the man admitted that he had originally requested the elephant from the prince with evil intent. The prince refused the offer and answered that he would not take back something he had given away. Finally he arrived at the palace.

The prince at the centre of this account was none other than our great teacher, Buddha Shakyamuni, in one of his previous lifetimes as a bodhisattva.

5

The Perfection of Morality

The second of the six perfections is the perfection of morality. Generally speaking, morality refers to the mental state which longs to discard nonvirtuous deeds. It is the foundation for practising patience, meditation and the other perfections. Since all the practices require discipline, the practice of moral discipline is necessary training for everything to follow. It is like preparing the soil to grow crops. When we later on engage in other virtuous actions, they will increase and multiply, and the flow of positive results will be incessant. On the other hand, without the support of moral discipline, we will not succeed in developing any of the other spiritual qualities.

The way to transform mundane morality into the perfection of morality is to engage in it with the motivation to liberate all sentient beings, conjoined with the Mahayana view of ultimate reality. When both the enlightenment thought and the Mahayana view of ultimate reality are conjoined with morality, it becomes the perfection of morality. Although ordinary worldlings and those on the Hinayana path also engage in morality, it is not possible for them to practise the perfection of morality, because they do not generate the enlightenment thought and they lack the Mahayana view of ultimate reality.

There are three ways in which our morality may be impaired:

(1) through not guarding the morality we have promised to maintain;

(2) through following the wrong type of morality, such as the morality of other religious traditions; and

(3) through practising the morality of the Hinayana path, which cannot become the cause for gaining full and perfect enlightenment.

The unfavourable consequence of impairing our morality, accruing in this lifetime, is that we will be criticized by the people around us. We will also feel ashamed even to appear before our teacher, to sit with other members of the sangha or to receive offerings. This is because when we know our morality is not pure, it instils a kind of cowardice or timidity within us. We will feel very small when we receive offerings. Not only will other people criticize and blame us, but nonhumans will also make obstacles for us. Gods who protected us in the past will no longer protect us, and buddhas and bodhisattvas will be displeased with us.

The unfavourable consequence accruing in the next life is rebirth in one of the lower realms. Unless we guard our morality properly, we will not be protected from taking birth there, even if we listen to the teachings and study them well. It is said that if we commit the ten nonvirtuous deeds, we will definitely be reborn in the lower realms. Even if we commit only some of the minor nonvirtues, this may also lead to rebirth there. Engaging in the moral practices of other religions will lead to rebirth within samsara. Practising the morality of the Hinayana may lead to nirvana, but this is only the nirvana of personal liberation. Since it is not the perfect and complete enlightenment, this nirvana has grave disadvantages.

There are four causes of impaired morality:

(1) being ignorant of the precepts of morality;

(2) not having proper devotion and respect for the rules of morality;

(3) heedlessness in maintaining morality; and

(4) being in the grip of manifold defilements.

Of these four, being in the grip of manifold defilements is the strongest impairment to our morality. We should be aware that there are two methods to overcome defilements:

(1) subduing the defilements individually as they arise; and
(2) discarding their seeds.

(1) Subduing the defilements individually as they arise

By this method, at the very instant we find ourselves in the grip of a certain manifested defilement such as anger, we should counteract it by reflecting on its opposite, loving-kindness and compassion. Similarly, if desire arises, we should counter it on the spot by reflecting on the ugliness or impure nature of the body. In such ways we can counteract defilements as they arise.

(2) Discarding their seeds

This can be achieved only by habituation in realizing selflessness. Bodhisattvas should engage in three kinds of morality:

(i) morality of discarding all nonvirtuous deeds;
(ii) morality of accumulating virtuous deeds; and
(iii) morality of performing deeds for the benefit of sentient beings.

(i) Morality of discarding all nonvirtuous deeds

There are two levels of morality which discard all nonvirtuous deeds: one level pertains to lay practitioners and the other to celibates. With regard to lay practitioners, there are five categories. The first is the layperson who takes the refuge vows. This person is known as an 'upasaka who maintains refuge in the Triple Gem.' A person who takes one of the four root precepts in addition to that,—for example, not committing murder—is known as an 'upasaka holding one precept.' One who maintains two of the five precepts is known as an 'upasaka observing some precepts.' One who maintains three of the five precepts is known as an 'upasaka observing most of the precepts.' One who maintains all four root vows and does not indulge in intoxicants is known as the 'complete upasaka.' Taking the five vows also includes upholding the ten virtuous deeds.[2] In other words, this precept holder must promise to discard the ten nonvirtuous deeds in addition to observing the five precepts.

According to certain Mahayana traditions, there is another level of lay practitioner who, in addition to taking the five basic vows, takes a vow of celibacy. This person is known as a brahmacharya or celibate upasaka, because he observes the pure morality of a celibate in addition to the other vows. There are also lay practitioners who take the eight precepts of upavasa, not just for one day but for their entire lives. These practitioners are known as 'gomi' upasakas. These two types of lay precept holders—the brahmacharya upasakas and the eight-precept holders—differ from other lay practitioners in that they observe the vow of celibacy. Of course, since they do not take all the vows of monks and nuns, they also differ from them. Whether we are lay practitioners or monks and nuns, provided we conjoin our vows with the Mahayana enlightenment thought (wishing to liberate all sentient beings), we will become holders of the pratimoksha or moral vow of the Mahayana. If on the other hand we take and maintain our vows with only our personal liberation in mind, our vows become Hinayana pratimoksha vows.

It is important to begin our practices with a vow, because otherwise they will not become the causes for any of the three liberations or enlightenments. As just described with regard to the pratimoksha vows, those on the Mahayana path may take the vows of a lay person, a monk or a nun through the rituals prescribed in the Hinayana teachings, as followed by the Hinayanists, and they may also take the bodhisattva vows through the ritual systems of either the Middle Way or the Mind-Only schools.

With regard to people who perform virtuous deeds without holding a vow of morality, their practice of virtue is weak and will

2　Upholding the ten virtuous deeds involves discarding the ten nonvirtuous deeds. The first three virtues are associated with actions of the body. These are (1) not killing; (2) not taking what has not been given; and (3) Refraining from improper sexual practices. There are four virtuous actions of speech: (4) not telling falsehoods; (5) not using abusive language; (6) not slandering others; and (7) not indulging in irrelevant talk or idle gossip. There are three virtuous actions of mind: (8) not being covetous; (9) not being malicious; and (10) not holding perverse views.

become a cause neither for liberation nor for Buddhahood. This means that, for example, if a person who has taken the vow of not killing produces the thought in his mind 'I will not kill any other person,' he produces the virtue of discarding killing every moment he is not engaged in the act of killing, because he is motivated by a mind seeking to abandon nonvirtue. However, one who simply lives his life without killing does not perform the virtue of discarding killing, because he does not possess a mind seeking to abandon killing. In brief, the mere failure to commit nonvirtuous acts does not produce virtue. We must therefore hold a vow of morality, which is the intention to discard nonvirtuous deeds. In this way, as long as we continue not to commit nonvirtuous deeds, we are actively engaging in virtue.

There are two ways of training in morality, the brief and the extensive. With regard to the brief, there are three divisions: object, time and nature. Of these three, the first is the practice of discarding nonvirtue in terms of object. In order to train in morality, it is necessary to begin in a small way with simple practices and then gradually expand our scope. We can do this from the viewpoint of the object. For example, we should begin our practice of discarding the ten nonvirtuous deeds with close family and friends. After becoming accustomed to this, we can expand our practice of 'discarding killing,' for example, to other human beings and animals. Likewise, with regard to discarding stealing, we should first practise with close relatives and neighbours and then extend this to include other people and finally to all sentient beings. This same method should be applied to discarding the remaining eight nonvirtuous deeds, such as telling lies and so forth.

From the perspective of time, one should first try to practise not committing any of these nonvirtuous deeds for half a day and gradually extend it to a full day, a week, a fortnight, then a full month and so on up to an entire year or more. We can also train from the viewpoint of nature of the deed, observing one vow in the beginning and then gradually increasing the number of vows we keep.

If for some reason we impair our morality, we must restore it immediately by confessing our misdeeds. If we commit an immoral deed in the morning, we must make sure we confess it before going to sleep that night. If we commit a nonvirtuous deed at night, we must confess it the next morning when we wake up, before taking any food. If we are always conscientious about confessing, we will become genuine Dharma practitioners. Buddha taught that there are two kinds of noble persons: those who never impair their morality and those who confess their infractions immediately.

(ii) Morality of accumulating virtuous deeds
The second practice of morality, which must be undertaken by bodhisattvas, is the accumulation of merit. The accumulation of merit means to practise morality and also to abandon unfavourable conditions which obstruct the accomplishment of virtuous deeds. For example, if we listen to Buddha's teachings or study them, this itself is a virtuous deed. If we find ourselves being obstructed by negative forces such as laziness, we must identify them and overcome them so we can continue our study vigorously. Abandoning negativities such as laziness is itself a virtuous deed and will improve our capacity for undertaking practices to accumulate merit, such as listening to the teachings and so forth. To give a further example, when we take refuge in the Triple Gem, it is possible that we may be obstructed by lack of faith. In order to overcome this, we must generate appropriate respect and devotion towards the Triple Gem by reflecting on their qualities. This becomes a virtuous deed in itself; it will strengthen our affirmation of the Triple Gem and add to our accumulation of merit. In brief, to collect or accumulate merit means not only performing virtuous deeds but also overcoming the negative forces which obstruct our performance of virtuous deeds.

(iii) Morality of performing deeds for the benefit of sentient beings
In order to work for the benefit of sentient beings, we must first overcome any unfavourable conditions which may impede us. For example, if an ordained Mahayana practitioner needs to transgress any of the four major vows in order to accomplish the greater benefit of sentient beings, he should do so, even if it means breaking his ordination vows.

With regard to unerringly undertaking the perfection of morality, there are four qualities to be adopted and seven attachments to be abandoned. These were explained previously in conjunction with the perfection of generosity. They apply to the perfection of morality and to all the other perfections.

There are many stories in the scriptures to illustrate how a bodhisattva must transgress the morality of discarding nonvirtuous deeds when it is necessary to do so for the benefit of sentient beings. Two of these stories will be mentioned here. The first is about a brahmin named Karma. He lived a very long time ago, in the days when people were able to live for thousands of years. This brahmin renounced the world and became a monk. He went to live in a forest to meditate, where he remained meditating very diligently and well for 4,200 years. After that time, he went to a nearby town and stayed in a king's palace. One day a trader's daughter came to the palace and saw him. She was very attracted to him and went to his room to ask him to marry her. The monk Karma told her that she should not speak of such a thing to him, as he had renounced the world. Then the girl replied that if he got up and walked away from her, she would kill herself the moment he took the seventh step. The monk thought to himself that he had renounced the world and taken vows, so he could not marry this girl. Thereupon he stood up and began to walk away. Then just as he was about to take the seventh step, he realized that if the girl were to kill herself in his room, it would be terrible for her and cause a great scandal. He then resolved that she should be an object of his great compassion and that he should break his vows to save her, even if it meant going to hell as a result. In other words, it was more important to save the girl than to save himself. Thus he turned back from taking the seventh step and accepted the girl as his wife.

After they had lived together for twelve years, he renounced the world again and went away to practise for a long time. It is said that he was reborn in a heavenly realm. This shows that instead of attaining a negative result through that deed, he accumulated a vast amount of merit by resolving to put someone else's benefit before his own. The brahmin Karma was the Buddha Shakyamuni in one of his previous lives.

The second story is about a ship's captain. At one time there were five hundred traders who had been sailing around the ocean and visiting many islands in search of jewels. Having had a highly successful trip, they embarked on their return journey. One of the ship's crew members, who had seen the traders' collection of riches, conceived a plan to kill them all and steal their jewels. The ship's captain became aware of this crew member's intention. As this captain was a man of great compassion, he tried to think of ways to prevent this deed. However, he could not think of a viable plan. He knew that if this evil man were to kill all the traders, he would be reborn in the hell realms for a very long time indeed. He felt compassion and thought to himself that if he were to kill the man before he could carry out his nefarious plan, he would save him from having to face such sufferings in the future. Therefore, with the intention of exchanging his own benefit and happiness for the suffering of others, the ship's captain killed the man. It is said that instead of being born in the hell realms, the captain accumulated a lot of merit, equivalent to what he would have accumulated through practising virtue for nine eons. Therefore instead of being a negative deed, this act of killing became a positive one. Again, this captain was Buddha Shakyamuni in one of his previous lives.

According to the Hinayana tradition, one must never at any time break the four principal vows of an ordained person: killing, stealing, sexual conduct and lying. It is said that one's spiritual life would be ruined by breaking any of these. However, according to the Mahayana tradition, provided that we are motivated by compassion and the enlightenment thought, we must break the four vows if it is necessary to do so to benefit others. There is no fault.

Benefits of maintaining morality

Maintaining morality conveys great benefits. First, with regard to the temporary benefits, we will never regret our actions in this life. Our mind will remain contented and we will attain various states of meditative absorption in addition to various realizations. Our conduct will bring joy to others, and they will revere us. We will even become fields of offering. In brief, many great benefits accrue from maintaining morality. Through maintaining our morality in this lifetime, we will be reborn in the higher realms of humans and gods and possess special qualities such as higher status, prosperity, wisdom, power, long life, beauty and freedom from diseases.

Second, the ultimate result of maintaining morality is the attainment of perfect Buddhahood. When we become Buddhas, our fame will spread widely. Everybody will call us 'teacher,' not only in the world of human beings but also in the world of the devas. In addition, by becoming a Buddha, we will also attain the quality of being free from the three concealments, as extolled by Arya Maitreya in *Mahayanasutralamkara*. Unlike worldly people, Buddha need not hide any of his behaviour of body, voice or mind to demonstrate that he is holy.

6

The Perfection of Patience

The perfection of patience is the third of the six perfections. Generally speaking, the practice of patience means not allowing the mind to become agitated by unfavourable circumstances or by the absence of favourable ones; for example, not becoming angry when someone does something harmful to us. If our practice of patience is carried out with the intention to rescue all sentient beings from the prison of cyclic existence, in conjunction with the correct view of ultimate reality, our practice becomes the Mahayana perfection of patience.

The opposing factor to patience is anger or hatred, which arises due to an unhappy mind. If we do not practise patience, our anger will lead to misfortune in this lifetime and, indeed, in many lifetimes to come. In this life itself, our body may be disturbed by anger to the point of illness, and our mind may become too disturbed for us to think properly. Consumed by angry thoughts of retaliation, we won't be able to sleep properly at night. If left unchecked, hatred and anger can drive us to insanity. An angry or short-tempered person is never trusted. Even if he brings gifts, the receiver may suspect he is being tricked or harmed in some way. Not even close relatives and friends will enjoy his company.

There are some who think getting angry can be beneficial, but this is incorrect. There is no time or place where anger can produce any benefit at all. A Dharma practitioner who acts angrily towards his teacher or towards other students won't even be regarded as a genuine practitioner and will not be wanted among the sangha. Even an ordinary householder who is full of hatred or anger will wreak havoc amongst his family members. Anger can break up marriages. Some couples become so embittered by anger that they refuse to communicate directly with each other and instead use their children as intermediaries.

Anger also results in great disadvantages in future lives. It is said that by just one moment of anger we can destroy the entire store of virtue accumulated over aeons. We may even be reborn in the hell realms. Therefore we should make every effort to overcome our anger. Two methods for overcoming anger and hatred are taught:

(1) overcoming the cause of anger; and
(2) producing the antidote to the cause of anger by working on anger directly once it has arisen.

(1) Overcoming the cause of anger

The cause of anger is an unhappy mind. By way of illustration, when someone harms us, our mind's first reaction is to become unhappy. Then on the basis of that unhappy mind, anger arises. That anger may in turn lead to unpleasant actions. So the basic cause of anger is unhappiness itself. Therefore, to prevent anger from arising, whenever we notice the mind sinking into an unhappy state, we should remind ourselves that an unhappy mind leads to anger. Furthermore, we should remind ourselves that an unhappy mind may destroy our entire accumulation of virtuous deeds. In fact, we cannot practise any virtuous deeds or accomplish any of our aims while our mind is unhappy. In summary, an unhappy mind is a source of immense suffering.

It is a good idea for us to recall all the disadvantages of generating an unhappy mind and falling under its power. For example, if we notice that our house is disintegrating into a state of dilapidation, there's no point in being unhappy about it. We can renovate it. Likewise, if we fall ill, instead of becoming miserable about it, we should look for a cure. If a problem can be remedied, we should turn our minds to fixing it. On the other hand, if a problem can't be remedied—say, our house has already fallen down, or we are about to die—it is pointless becoming depressed about it, because nothing can be done. We might as well just accept it. Whatever the circumstances, becoming unhappy solves nothing; it just produces more suffering and leads to even more serious misdeeds and still further suffering in the future.

The great Buddhist saint Shantideva emphasized that in order to overcome anger, we need to remove its cause, the unhappy mind. In brief, if we see our mind becoming unhappy, we must take measures to halt the process immediately. Otherwise, it will lead only to anger, and when anger arises it achieves nothing apart from causing further suffering for ourselves and others.

(2) Producing the antidote to the cause of anger by working on anger directly once it has arisen

The second method for overcoming anger is to work on it directly when it arises, by practising its antidote, patience. There are three kinds of patience we must engage in:

(i) patience of enduring sufferings;

(ii) patience of definitely considering the three factors from the viewpoints of the two truths; and

(iii) patience of not considering the other as 'harmer.'

(i) Patience of enduring sufferings

'Patience of enduring sufferings' means to accept sufferings gladly when they arise, instead of becoming irritated by them. We should remind ourselves that we are on the Mahayana path, and therefore we should always be thinking mostly about benefiting other sentient beings, not just about our own comfort. We should remember that other beings are the same as we are. They want happiness, just as we do. Likewise, they wish to avoid suffering, just as we do. We should always recall that we are working for the full and perfect enlightenment of all sentient beings, and since this is such a huge undertaking, we must be prepared to face hardships. We should remind ourselves of the magnitude of our commitment. Then we won't need to fear any type of suffering. When suffering does arise, as it inevitably will, instead of becoming unhappy or angry, we should generate a joyful mind. We should be content in the knowledge of the great purpose we are accomplishing by our aim to bring all beings to happiness and ultimately complete enlightenment. In brief, practising 'the patience of enduring sufferings' involves transforming dissatisfied or unhappy physical and mental states into favourable conditions in order to enhance our spiritual practice.

(ii) Patience of definitely considering the three factors from the viewpoints of the two truths

There are two ways of practising this second method to counteract anger: one is from the perspective of relative truth and the other is from the perspective of ultimate truth. From the relative perspective, it is plain to see that the nature of the fire element is heat, the nature of the water element is fluidity, the nature of the earth element is solidity and the nature of the air element is movement. In the same way, the nature of cyclic existence is suffering. As we are part of this world, it follows that it is our nature to experience suffering. We should also understand that it is our nature as sentient beings to harm each other, due to our selfish desire for our own benefit. In brief, based on the understanding that the nature of this world is suffering, that it is our nature to experience suffering and that it is the nature of sentient beings to bring about suffering in each other, we can subdue anger and practise patience.

We are all familiar with the behaviour known as causing self-harm. These days we often read about people who commit suicide by jumping off a cliff, shooting themselves or whatever, perhaps just because a business deal failed. But we may not always be aware that the harm we do to others is really self-harm, because it will result in similar harm being done to us in the future. Therefore if someone harms us now, it is because we must have done something against him in the past. We are simply being repaid for negative deeds performed in previous lifetimes. In fact, most of our actions are nonvirtuous; it is as a result of our past actions that we have been born into this world to experience the sufferings of birth, old age, sickness and death. Since we ourselves create great suffering by carrying out nonvirtuous deeds, it is we who are harming ourselves.

In brief, with this understanding, we can see that the person who appears to be harming us is not the principal cause of our suffering. Our present sufferings arise mainly from our past misdeeds. Therefore there is no point in becoming angry with someone who may appear to be harming us. The harm he does us is a small matter compared with the great harm we are doing to ourselves all the time. If we really understand this, we will not produce a retaliatory attitude. In fact, we will not even see another person's 'harmful' actions as being harmful to us in any way.

Here is a story to illustrate the correct practice of patience. One day Buddha Shakyamuni asked if one of his disciples would go to another place to teach the Dharma. An arhat disciple volunteered to go. Buddha warned him that this was not a very pleasant place, as the followers there were very angry people. Then he asked the arhat what he would do if the people there caused him trouble. The arhat replied that he would not do anything at all, just practise patience. Then Buddha asked him what he would do if someone abused him. The arhat replied that he would not do anything at all, just practise patience. Next Buddha asked him what he would do if the people threw stones at him. The arhat responded that it would be very kind of the people just to throw stones at him, because they could kill him instead. He said that he would just be thankful they didn't lead him down into the hell realms. Buddha was then satisfied and instructed his disciple to proceed to that place.

To practise patience through proper understanding from the ultimate viewpoint means that when someone is doing something harmful to us, we should examine carefully to find out whether the person doing the harm, we ourselves or the act of harm actually exist. We will discover that from the ultimate viewpoint, none of these three has any reality. As all three lack inherent nature from the perspective of that higher logical mind, there is absolutely no need for us to become angry. This is another way of pacifying anger.

(iii) Patience of not considering the other as 'harmer'

The third category of practising patience is to avoid producing any thought of anger against the person who harms us (or appears to do so). For example, if someone commits some harmful action against us, we must not even think that a harmful action is being done. We must instead remember that the person who appears to be doing us harm was our mother or our child over many past lifetimes. In this way, we will think of the person with loving-kindness instead of anger.

We should also realize that whoever appears to harm us is actually offering us the opportunity to develop patience. For example, just as we cannot take the refuge vow unless there is someone such as an abbot to bestow it, neither can we practise patience without someone causing (or appearing to cause) us harm. In this sense then, there is absolutely no difference between our spiritual friend, from whom we receive the vow, and the person who causes us harm. Both enable us to accumulate virtue. So the one who harms us is really our great benefactor and is therefore the equal of our spiritual friend who helps us practise the path. That being the case, when we feel we are about to be 'harmed' we should generate great joy, like a criminal sentenced to execution who is reprieved at the last moment and has his hand cut off instead. In brief, when we practise patience towards 'harmful' people, we purify negative karma, which might otherwise propel us to rebirth in the hell realms.

Another approach is to bear in mind that anyone who tries to harm us will have to endure great hardships. He will have to come in search of us and get hold of a weapon and so on. In addition, he will accumulate a lot of nonvirtuous karma, which will cause him great suffering in the future. We should therefore generate compassion towards him. If we cannot actually manage to generate compassion, at least we should avoid producing anger. We should understand that those who try to harm us are acting under the sway of the defilements: desire, anger and ignorance. So it is not really the other person who is doing the harm. The harm is really being committed by the defilements, over which he has no control! For these reasons, we must generate compassion instead of anger towards those who appear to harm us.

We should begin to train in the practice of patience gradually, starting with those closest to us, such as our loved ones. Once we can practise patience towards them, we should extend our practice to people slightly further removed, such as friends or acquaintances. When we can manage to be patient with them, we should expand the practice still further to beings we do not know, such as mosquitoes which bite us. We should gradually expand the scope of our patience until we include our greatest enemies. With regard to time, we should begin with short periods and gradually build up. We might begin by promising ourselves to practise patience for half a day and then for a day and so on. If even that is too long, we can begin with maybe half an hour and then an hour and keep on extending the period until it embraces our entire lifetime. We should also practise patience progressively with respect to the degree of harm we feel is being done to us. As the harm inflicted on us seems to be greater if we are cowardly by nature, we should try to extend our act of patience by degrees to greater and greater kinds of sufferings, beginning with minor harms like a mosquito bite and extending to diseases and other physical and mental sufferings.

We should understand that great advantages will accrue from our study and training in patience, if it is carried out to enhance our practice and enable us to achieve our goals. On the other hand, if we try to do it for other reasons, we will not receive blessings and will not be able to accomplish what we wish. For example, if someone studies the Dharma primarily in order to write about it and teach others for this life's gain, without understanding the Doctrine properly, he will not receive the blessings of Dharma and will not accomplish the path. However, if we practise patience with the understanding that we are doing it in order to progress on the path to enlightenment, we will certainly receive the blessings.

In order to transform our practice of patience into the perfection of patience, we must conjoin it with the four positive qualities and abandon the seven attachments. The four positive qualities of patience are:

(1) all forms of anger must be relinquished;

(2) it must be associated with the nonconceptual realization of ultimate reality – selflessness of persons and phenomena;

(3) by relying on patience, we must work to fulfil others' wishes; and

(4) by relying on patience, we must work to ripen sentient beings by placing them on one of the three yanas, in accordance with their temporary race.

If we can conjoin all four of these qualities within a single act of patience, we are practising the perfection of patience correctly. To elaborate briefly on this, by not producing hatred or anger when someone harms us, we accomplish the first quality. If that is conjoined with the realization of the ultimate state of being of the three factors of patience, the second quality is present. By not deliberately retaliating, we have fulfilled the harmer's wishes. Thus the third quality is present. He may also be a little surprised by our response. His wish to harm us may be transformed into a feeling of warmth, friendship and curiosity. He may even approach us and ask us to explain our attitude. Then we can lead him onto the path of Dharma. Thus the fourth quality is fulfilled. If all four qualities are present in this one act of patience, it becomes the perfection of patience.

While practising patience, we must also abandon the seven attachments, which are as follows.

(1) Attachment to anger, the opposite of patience.

(2) Attachment to postponement, the idea that we can retaliate now and practise patience later on. We should abandon such a thought; patience should be practised right at the moment when the harm is being inflicted on us.

(3) Attachment to being satisfied with the amount of patience we are practising. An example of this is when someone harms us and we exercise just a little patience, feeling satisfied that it is enough, or feeling that we should exert patience just for a few minutes and then retaliate. We should never be satisfied with the amount of patience we are practising, and we should keep on increasing the amount.

(4) Attachment to the expectation of some reward in this lifetime. For example, when someone does harm to us, we might think that by being patient with him he will like us or reward us.

(5) Attachment to expecting positive results in future lives. We should abandon any hope of reward and just practise patience in order to accumulate virtue.

(6) Attachment to any inclination to factors opposing patience, in this case the disposition towards anger.

(7) Attachment to the two distractions: the distraction of speculation, which means to take pleasure in the lower vehicle, and the distraction of conceptual thought, which means to have a conceptual attachment to the three factors of the act of practising patience (the recipient of harm, the harmer and the act of patience itself).

The benefits of practising patience

When we examine the benefits of practising patience, we will see that there are benefits both in this lifetime and in future lifetimes. For example, in this lifetime, by not reacting angrily towards someone who harms us, we can calm the person down. We will decrease the level of violence against us even if we do not stop it completely. That means we will gradually be able to pacify all our enemies, and thereby they will cease to be enemies. Then there will be no need to worry about others harming us. We will be fearless even at the time of death. In future lives, as a result of practising patience, we will gain a beautiful body, long life, freedom from sickness and many rebirths in positions of high status, such as that of a king or a god in the heavenly realms. We will also be free from enemies in future lives. With regard to the ultimate benefits, when we become a fully enlightened Buddha, we will possess the thirty-two major and eighty minor marks, which instil great joy in all who perceive them.

7

The Perfection of Enthusiasm
or Joyous Effort

The fourth perfection, the perfection of enthusiasm or joyous effort, is defined as the mental state which takes joy in virtue. If our enthusiasm is motivated by the wish to liberate all sentient beings from the prison of cyclic existence, conjoined with the Mahayana view of ultimate reality, our practice becomes the perfection of enthusiasm.

The forces opposed to the perfection of enthusiasm are:

(1) laziness of not engaging in virtuous deeds through body, speech and mind;

(2) laziness of although being ostensibly engaged, striving diligently to cultivate deeds which are not virtuous deeds, while taking them to be virtuous, as the Indian heretics do; and

(3) laziness of putting effort into virtuous deeds which result in the extremes of worldly existence and 'minor' liberation.

A disadvantage of laziness is being unable to accomplish even ordinary worldly objectives, let alone the spiritual activities of listening, contemplating and meditating. If we attempt to practise the spiritual path without enthusiasm, we will never accomplish the result. Furthermore, if we are lazy in our practice, results gained in previous lifetimes may be lost.

When people are feeling lazy, they may think that some kind of demon is obstructing them and causing the laziness. However, Buddha said that laziness itself is the demon; there is no outside force causing it. So whenever we find ourselves slipping into laziness, we should call to mind the following:

- laziness is the greatest obstacle of all to accomplishing the path of Dharma;
- Buddha said that without enthusiasm we will never be able to accomplish even our own purpose, let alone the purpose of helping other sentient beings; and
- in a sutra it is said that unless we possess enthusiasm, we cannot accomplish the practice of the other perfections.

Causes of laziness

Before we look at the methods for overcoming laziness we must first look at its causes, which were taught by Shri Shantideva in the *Bodhicharyavatara*:

(1) Being attached to postponing activities.

(2) Being attached to other types of work, such as worldly activities, trade or farming; in other words, having no desire to perform virtue and taking no joy in its performance.

(3) Being in a state of slothfulness through discouragement, because although one has been engaged in the practice of virtuous deeds for some time, one has not accomplished what one wished.

(4) The laziness of belittling oneself, thinking, 'One such as I could never perform such virtuous deeds.'

(5) Not engaging in virtuous deeds because of just lying around and relaxing.

(6) Being attached to enjoying worldly pleasures such as eating, drinking, gossiping, etc.

(7) Not engaging in virtue because of spending day and night asleep.

(8) Not feeling aversion towards samsara, meaning that we do not understand the faults of samsara or the faults of working for this life alone.

It is apparent that most of the causes of laziness arise from our attachment to working for the sake of this life alone.

Methods for overcoming laziness

The most effective immediate antidote for overcoming laziness is to reflect again and again on impermanence. We should reflect that this life will not last very long. My own teacher, Deshung Ajam Rinpoche, once told me that being greatly attached to this life creates immense obstacles. He was referring to himself. He said that because he was so attached to this life, he could not benefit himself in any way. When we are strongly attached to this life, there is no possibility of maturing our minds in order to carry out genuine spirituality. We cannot turn our mind away from worldliness and hence cannot bring benefit even to ourselves. One who truly wants to practise Dharma must feel aversion towards this life's aims and ambitions.

By way of illustration, it is said that there was a Kadampa monk who thought he was practising Dharma very diligently. One day, while he was circumambulating a temple, a great teacher by the name of Geshe Tonpa approached him and remarked that while performing circumambulations was excellent, it would really be better for him to practise Dharma. The Kadampa monk thought to himself that studying the scriptures must surely count as practising Dharma, so he started studying the scriptures. Geshe Tonpa again came to up him and said that what he was doing was excellent, but that it would be better still to practise Dharma. The monk thought that meditating might be the way to practise Dharma, so he embarked on the practice of meditation with great enthusiasm. Again, Geshe Tonpa came to him and said that while practising meditation was indeed excellent, would it not be better if he practised Dharma? Hearing this again, the Kadampa monk asked him how Dharma should be practised. Geshe Tonpa replied that the way to practise Dharma was to give up attachment to this life.

When we think about how Dharma must be practised, it may be likened to a meeting. If we called a meeting of many people and the chairman failed to show up, the meeting would be unsuccessful. Likewise, while one is practising there are indeed many virtuous thoughts in the mind, but if the understanding of the impermanence of this life is not present, our practice will be unsuccessful. While we are totally engaged in worldly activities and our mind is attached to the eight worldly dharmas (gain and loss, fame and disgrace, praise and blame, pleasure and misery), no matter what deeds we perform, they cannot be virtuous deeds. Of course, as long as we remain within samsara, it is impossible for us to abandon these eight worldly Dharmas completely. Nevertheless, if we perform deeds with the understanding of the need to reduce or abandon our attachment to these eight, we are entering the Dharma.

It is pure folly to be attached to this life, thinking that it is permanent. We should see that this life is short and we have no idea when we will leave it. By being attached to it, we are only creating obstacles for ourselves. Take as an example someone embarked on a long journey, who after having travelled for quite a while, decides to stop and rest. If he were to build an entire house to rest in, that would be a mistake, because he still has a long way to go. Similarly, if we worked just for this life alone, it would be akin to stopping and building a house we don't need, as we will soon be leaving it. Therefore it is a grave error not to keep in mind the impermanence of this life, and it is futile to work for the sake of this life alone.

Enthusiasm itself is the remedy for laziness. There are two aspects of this:

(1)   purifying the spheres of activity; and
(2)   practising excellence.

(1) Purifying the spheres of activity

Purifying the spheres of activity means that in addition to adopting virtuous deeds and refraining from nonvirtuous deeds, we should transform all our neutral actions into virtuous deeds. When sitting at home, the bodhisattva should form the resolution, 'May I reach the city of liberation.' Likewise when going to sleep, he or she should resolve, 'May I attain the Dharmakaya of Buddhahood.' If he dreams, 'May I realize that every phenomenon is like a dream.' When waking up, 'May I awaken from ignorance.' When rising, 'May I attain the form body of Buddhahood.' When dressing, 'May I put on the robe of self-respect and shame.' When tying up one's belt, 'May my mind be connected to the roots of merit.' When sitting on a mat, 'May I attain the adamantine seat at the stage of awakening.'

When resting one's back against something, 'May I arrive at the tree under which awakening is attained.' When lighting a fire, 'May the defilements be burned up.' When the fire is burning, 'May the fire of transcendental wisdom blaze forth.' When food is being prepared, 'May I attain the ambrosia of transcendental wisdom.' When eating, 'May I acquire the food of meditative concentration.'

When going outside, 'May I escape from the city of cyclic existence.' When going downstairs, 'May I enter into cyclic existence for the benefit of sentient beings.' When opening a door, 'May the gate to the city of liberation be opened.' When closing a door, 'May the door to the three miserable destinies be shut.' When embarking on a path, 'May I enter upon the noble path.' When going uphill, 'May sentient beings be established in the happiness of the higher destinies.' When going downhill, 'May the continuum of the three lower destinies be broken.'

When meeting another sentient being, 'May I meet the completely awakened Buddha.' When placing one's foot on the ground, 'May I place my trust in accomplishing the welfare of all sentient beings.' When raising one's foot, 'May all sentient beings be brought forth from cyclic existence.' When seeing someone wearing ornaments, 'May I gain the marks and auspicious characteristics of a Buddha.' When seeing someone not wearing ornaments, 'May I come to possess the excellent qualities of a purified person.' If one sees a full vessel, 'May I be filled with excellent qualities.' If one sees an empty vessel, 'May I be devoid of all faults.' If one sees many happy beings, 'May I delight in the religious teachings.' If one sees people who are unhappy, 'May I not delight in any compounded thing.' If one sees a sentient being feeling pleasure, 'May I be equipped for the bliss of Buddhahood.' If one sees beings suffering, 'May the sufferings of all beings be pacified.' If one sees a sick person, 'May all sentient beings be free from every disease.' If one sees an attractive being, 'May all beings be attractive to the eyes of all the buddhas and bodhisattvas.' If one sees an ugly body, 'May beings not feel devotion towards evil teachers.'

On seeing someone being grateful for the kindness of another, 'May I repay the kindness of the buddhas and bodhisattvas.' If one sees someone who is ungrateful, 'May none be indebted to wrong views.' If one sees an ordained person, 'May I enter into the Noble Dharma.' If one sees someone undergoing hardships, 'May I be able

to endure hardships for the sake of the Noble Teachings.' If one sees
a person wearing armour, 'May I gird myself in order to undertake
the quest for the Noble Teachings.' If one sees a person without
armour, 'May I not gird myself for the pursuit of evil deeds.' If one
sees a person being aggressive, 'May all attackers be defeated.' If one
sees a sentient being praised, 'May all the buddhas and bodhisattvas
be praised.'

When one sees a city, 'May I see the city of liberation.' When
one sees a forest, 'May I become a place of resort for the whole
world, including the gods.' When the Dharma is being taught, 'May I
attain inexhaustible confidence to teach the Buddha's Doctrine.'
When crossing water, 'May I cross over the ocean of cyclic
existence.' When washing, 'May my body and mind be without
stain.' During hot weather, 'May the torments of the defilements be
soothed.' In cold weather, 'May I attain the coolness of extinction.'
When a religious discourse is being given, 'May I receive all the
teachings of a Buddha.' Whenever one sees a figure of the Buddha,
'May I acquire unobscured eyes to see all the buddhas.' When one
sees a stupa, 'May I become a shrine of worship for all beings.' When
looking, 'May I become worthy of being looked upon by the world
of humans and gods.' When physically paying homage, 'May I obtain
the head protuberance of a Buddha, with dimensions such that gods
and men cannot perceive it by looking.' When circumambulating,
'May I attain that which leads to the qualities of omniscience.' When
some are approaching the excellent qualities of Buddha, 'May I bring
to perfection the excellent, inexhaustible qualities.'

One should devise other suitable examples. When one sees
people engaging in trade, one should resolve, 'May I attain the seven
kinds of wealth of the aryas.'[3] When fields are being watered and
fertilized, resolve, 'May the crop of the thought of awakening be
plentiful.' When sowing seeds, 'May all sentient beings be implanted
with the seed of the thought of awakening.' When oxen are being
yoked together, 'May method be conjoined with discriminative
wisdom.' At the time of ploughing the fields, 'May the hard soil of
the defilements be broken up.' When weeding, 'May the weeds of
the defilements be uprooted.' During the harvest, 'May the crop of

3   The seven kinds of wealth of the aryas are faith, morality, hearing,
     generosity, sense of shame, dread of blame and wisdom.

gnosis be gathered.' When the grain is being threshed, 'May the obscurations, together with all their propensities, be removed.' When the grain is being washed, 'May I attain the fruit of complete Buddhahood.' When climbing a ladder, 'May I accomplish the ten bhumis stage by stage.' When arriving at a house, 'May I arrive at the stage of a perfectly awakened Buddha.' And so forth. For a more detailed account, one should consult the *Discourse on Purified Objects of Experience.*

In this way we can purify our ordinary actions, which by their nature are neither virtuous nor nonvirtuous, into virtuous deeds. If possible, we should consult other teachings about transforming the entire day into a day of virtue. We should study them carefully and to put them into practice.

(2) Practising excellence

The practice of excellence involves undertaking all our actions for the benefit of both ourselves and other sentient beings. Both aspects are taught in all the Buddhist · paths, although there are slight differences in emphasis. For example, in Hinayana, the primary purpose of engaging in spiritual practices is to accomplish benefits for ourselves, and the secondary purpose is to benefit others. In Mahayana, on the other hand, the primary purpose is to accomplish others' benefit. As a by-product, there will be benefits for ourselves as well.

When we engage in practising the six perfections, there are two ways of benefiting others: the direct method and the indirect method. For example, if we safeguard our money and possessions in order to give them away to others, we are working for others indirectly. When we actually give our things to them, we are working for others directly. As a by-product of practising these direct and indirect methods of working for the benefit of others, we also obtain benefits. For example, through the actual practice of generosity, we gain comfort and fame, and we will attract an excellent circle of followers in this lifetime and achieve prosperity in future lifetimes. Eventually we will accomplish the perfection of generosity and then the stages of enlightenment. So by working for the sake of others, we also accomplish benefits for ourselves. When we study the Doctrine for the sake of others, we are working indirectly for others' benefit, whereas when we teach others what we have understood in order to dispel their ignorance, we are working directly for their benefit. By mastering the religious teachings and applying them in order to help others, one will be happy in the present life and be counted among the ranks of the greatly wise. One will overwhelm all opponents and be trusted by everyone, even by the gods. In future lives one will achieve discriminating wisdom regarding each and every knowable thing. Further, as one will be reborn with skill in means, one's discriminating wisdom will be perfected.

When we practise virtue, we must be in a happy mood and enjoy what we do. Otherwise we will not be able to accomplish virtuous deeds. Even when it comes to worldly matters such as professional work, we won't be effective unless we are happy in our work. We will be miserable, not to mention the effect we will have on the people around us! However, if we enjoy what we do, we can succeed. Likewise, if we undertake study or a meditation retreat with a happy mind, we will be successful. As explained earlier, when practising the perfection of enthusiasm or joyous effort, we must conjoin it with the four positive qualities and abandon the seven attachments. The practice of the perfection of enthusiasm is also crucial to those following the Vajrayana path.

The benefits of practising enthusiasm

There are great benefits to be gained from practising enthusiasm. In this lifetime alone, we will be able to accomplish all the worldly and spiritual activities. We will attract followers, wealth and marvellous qualities. By obtaining wealth and acquisitions in harmony with religion, we will be happy in the present life and have no regrets when we die. Neither humans nor nonhumans will be able to obstruct our Dharma practice. We will gain knowledge and wisdom even in this lifetime. With regard to benefits in future lives, we will be able to relinquish nonvirtuous thoughts and accomplish virtuous thoughts in a short period of time. So we can see that all the purities and all the accomplishments arise from enthusiasm. Thus enthusiasm is the very source of accomplishing both worldly and supramundane qualities. Without enthusiasm it would be impossible to gain these qualities, just as movement would be impossible without the presence of the wind element. Therefore the practice of enthusiasm is indispensable. With regard to the ultimate result, the qualities resulting from the practice of enthusiasm at the stage of Buddhahood are the ten powers and the four kinds of fearlessness and so on, and Buddha's activities for the sake of sentient beings, which are accomplished without obstruction.

8

The Perfection of Meditative Concentration

The fifth of the six perfections is the perfection of meditative concentration. Meditative concentration refers to a mental state abiding one-pointedly on a single virtuous object, after discursive thoughts have been pacified. When this state of concentration is motivated by the Mahayana enlightenment thought and associated with the correct realization of ultimate reality, it becomes the perfection of concentration. On the other hand, even though our mind may be concentrated one-pointedly, if we meditate on the wrong view—for example, the views of other philosophies or religions—we won't achieve the main objective of our practice. If we seek a result only for this life, or seek only our own personal liberation, then even if we meditate in the correct manner with the proper understanding of the procedure, it will not be the perfection of meditative concentration.

The opposing force to concentration is distraction, the wavering or distracted mind. We cannot accomplish anything properly if our mind is distracted. Just as a stream of water will overflow and rush off in many directions if it lacks a suitable conduit, our thoughts flow out in many directions when our mind is distracted. Furthermore, just as water always flows downhill and forms a waterfall unless properly channelled, when our mind is not directed properly, it moves downward in a negative direction, seeking nonvirtuous thoughts and actions. Therefore it is a great fault not to be able to focus the mind properly in this lifetime. If we have not been able to achieve concentration properly, we will experience great regret and depression at the time of death. Thus it is manifestly evident that a distracted mind causes us to undergo great mental suffering. In future lives too, even if we make the effort to meditate, our mind will easily fall prey to distraction, and we will not be successful in overcoming it. Just as it is difficult to halt a river once it starts cascading over a cliff, it will be very difficult for us to curb the habit of distraction in future lifetimes. And if we cannot control distractions in future lifetimes, more and more nonvirtuous deeds will accumulate. Due to the ever-increasing store of defilements and unwholesome deeds, we will be reborn again and again in the lower realms. Further, if we meditate with the wrong view, it will create many obstacles. Thus it is essential to have proper knowledge of the methods of meditation, the goal of meditation and the view with which we engage in meditation. In this regard, it is narrated that there was once a Hindu practitioner who, after meditating for twelve years on a concept of emptiness which was not a proper view of ultimate reality, passed away and was reborn as a cat.

When we go somewhere and mistakenly take the wrong path, our journey will take longer because we will have to return to the start. In the same way, it is necessary to establish the proper understanding before we embark on the practice of meditation, so that we don't mistakenly follow the wrong path. According to the great Bodhisattva Maitreya, if we know that someone is mediating without having established the proper understanding, we should not criticize him or feel that we are in competition with him. Instead we should extend compassion to him, because he is going the wrong way.

It is said that if we carry on meditating only on loving-kindness or compassion and do not conjoin it with the correct wisdom of ultimate reality, we will never gain complete freedom from sufferings. Although meditation on loving-kindness and compassion is a virtuous practice, it is not a complete Mahayana path unless it is conjoined with the correct view of ultimate reality. Conversely, if we meditate just on the correct wisdom of ultimate reality without associating it with great compassion, it will not be a complete Mahayana path either. This is because, although we can gain a result such as the liberation of the lower vehicle, we cannot accomplish the greater benefit of others. Therefore, in order to engage properly in the Mahayana practice, we must conjoin both compassion and the correct realization of the ultimate state of being (in other words, we must conjoin method and wisdom).

With regard to the antidotes for overcoming distractions, there are two kinds:

(1) methods for overcoming the causes of distraction (antidotes to the cause); and

(2) methods for overcoming distractions directly (antidotes to the resultant distraction).

(1) Methods for overcoming the causes of distraction

With regard to overcoming the causes of the distracted mind, we must first identify them. Basically, our mind becomes distracted because of desirous attachment, especially attachment to other beings and to wealth. In order to overcome actual distraction, we must abandon such attachments.

(i) Overcoming attachment to other beings

It is obvious that there are many faults associated with being attached to others. First of all, attachment obstructs us from understanding the sufferings of worldly existence. If we fail to realize that worldly existence is a state of suffering, we won't wish to renounce it. If we become attached to others, we will suffer when we have to part with them. Furthermore, we will fall under their influence. Then instead of using our precious human rebirth, attained with such difficulty, for a worthwhile purpose, we will waste our life trying to satisfy the short-term, worldly desires of others. This becomes a serious obstacle to attaining the state of enlightenment. Furthermore, the people of this world are very hard to please; they become either happy or unhappy over trifling matters. At certain times they befriend us and at other times they turn into our enemies. When we do nice things for people with the thought of pleasing them, they may become displeased instead. They may even become angry and hate us for it. From all angles, it is extremely difficult to please others.

There are many problems in dealing with human beings: those at a lower level become jealous, those on the same level try to compete with us and those in higher positions look down on us arrogantly. If we praise people, they become proud. If we criticize them, they become resentful. Regardless of our relationships with others and irrespective of what we do to help them, we cannot be of any benefit to them at all. It is said that a wealthy person is criticized for what he has and a poor person is criticized for having nothing. In other words, everybody will be criticized, regardless of his position in life. In one sutra Buddha stated that all the inhabitants of this world are concerned only about their own benefit, and they become displeased when they don't get what they want. This being the case, there is no one in this world we can regard as a real friend.

We cannot place any reliance on the people of this world. If we are powerful, people will listen to us and respect us regardless of what we say, either because they fear us or because they hope to gain some advantage. But once we lose our power, people won't listen to us anymore, however inspiring our speech and however many favours we may have done them in the past; in fact, they'll criticize us. When we are wealthy, there will be lots of friends hanging around, pleased to do whatever they can for us; but when we lose our wealth, they will turn away from us, and we may never see their faces again. Buddha mentioned that although the Buddhist teachings are perfect in every way, some people nevertheless criticize them. Even Buddha himself was criticized during his time on earth. So if we think we can please everybody and hope that they will like us and look up to us, we are making a big mistake. We will never be able to satisfy the myriad people in this world, all of whom are constantly seeking different things.

At one time Buddha's cousin, Devadatta, who was also considered by ordinary people to be Buddha's great enemy, became ill and was nearing death. Buddha went to bless him, and he recovered. When Devadatta was well again, he showed great disrespect towards Buddha by telling him that the only reason he had been able to help him was that he was a capable doctor and added that because of his medical skills, he would have no problem feeding himself in his old age!

Also during the time of Buddha, there was a man by the name of Lekpay Karma (Su nachetra) who told Buddha that a Jain master had gained the state of omniscience, and that he was the only one in the world who possessed this quality. Buddha told Lekpay Karma that the Jain master would die of indigestion in seven days' time. Lekpay

Karma went back to the Jain master and told him what Buddha had said. He advised the master to eat very little during the next seven days to prove Buddha wrong. So the Jain master ate hardly any food for six days. However, he miscalculated and thought that the next day, which was actually the seventh day, was the eighth. So he ate a good meal and died of indigestion on the seventh day. He was reborn as a hungry ghost. In the form of this hungry ghost rebirth, the Jain master met Lekpay Karma and told him that Buddha had been correct. Buddha was the real omniscient one, he said, and Lekpay Karma should give up his disbelief in Buddha, seek his blessings and take refuge in him. Nevertheless, Lekpay Karma did not like this idea, and he did not develop faith in Buddha. In fact, when he met Buddha later on, he told him that he had been wrong to say that the Jain master would die, because the Jain master had not died. Buddha replied, 'Not only did your teacher, the Jain master, die within seven days, but he has actually spoken to you in the form of his rebirth as a hungry ghost.' Lekpay Karma retorted that Buddha was mistaken about the Jain master having been reborn as a hungry ghost, because he had actually been reborn in one of the heavenly realms. Buddha asked, 'Then who was that hungry ghost you were just talking to, who told you to come and see me and to have faith in me?' At that point Lekpay Karma realized that Buddha really had omniscience. He became highly embarrassed and ashamed about having tried to trick him. Nonetheless, although he now understood that Buddha had the quality of omniscience and could see the future and the state of other beings, he still did not develop faith in him. Even though he saw the power of Buddha, he just walked away. This account shows that although Buddha is completely omniscient and perfectly enlightened, even he cannot satisfy every living being.

Furthermore, Buddha said that we should not be attached even to our loved ones, such as parents or close relatives, because eventually we will have to part with them. When we exit this life, we will be on our own. No one can help us then, not even those who have helped us during this lifetime. Furthermore, it is not appropriate to hate our enemies, because everybody is always changing. Even friends and loved ones can become enemies during this life, not to mention future lifetimes. Here is a story to illustrate this point. There was a couple who had a daughter. The husband was later reborn as a fish and the wife as a dog. At one time the daughter was sitting by the roadside, eating a fish with her baby on her lap. While she was eating, a dog tried to get the bone from her. She beat and kicked the dog. As she sat holding the baby, munching the fish and driving the dog away, an arhat passed by. Looking at them through his clairvoyance, he shook his head and murmured to himself that the world was a very strange place indeed. The woman was eating her father, beating her mother and sitting with her enemy resting on her lap. Thus we can see how futile it is to become attached to others in this life!

(ii) Overcoming attachment to wealth

Another major cause of distraction is attachment to wealth and possessions. In order to accumulate material riches, we engage in nonvirtue and encounter great difficulties. In all three phases of acquiring things—trying to gain them, having gained them and then losing them—suffering is always involved. For example, at the time of trying to accumulate wealth, we have to do a lot of difficult things and commit many nonvirtuous actions. Sometimes we even have to speak violently. We may cheat others or take advantage of them. In the process, even those who are close to us become our enemies, and our enemies are further alienated. So at every stage of accumulating and guarding wealth, we commit many unwholesome deeds out of desirous attachment. Therefore we are unable to travel the path leading to supreme bliss. Once we obtain possessions, we suffer through fear of losing them and we suffer still more trying to protect them. Our worry about protecting our possessions becomes so great that we become slaves to them. Instead of being owned by us, they begin to own us. We have to work for them. We create many enemies in our attempts to protect our things from others. We fear that others may try to take our things, and we therefore begin to mistrust people. Due to always trying to protect our belongings, we generate negative thoughts and perform negative deeds which cause our defilements to multiply, leading to a never-ending cycle of suffering. Similarly, when we lose things, we become unhappy and displeased with others, and this generates hatred and anger. Consequently we cannot practise virtue, and our store of merit is soon exhausted. This in turn produces further defilements, sufferings and nonvirtuous deeds. However, this does not mean we have to throw away everything we own. Possessions themselves are not the problem. The fault is with our attachment to them; this is what we need to overcome. So there is no need for you to toss your car keys away right now and catch a bus home! Similarly, when we are attached to other living beings, it does not mean there is something wrong with them. The problem lies in our desirous attachment itself. Other people are all right as they are, but we must overcome our attachment to them, just as we must overcome or at least reduce our attachment to possessions. This will help us defeat distractions.

When it is asked whether we can gain any happiness at all through possessions, the answer is that they may bring us some happiness in this life. Indeed, if we lack possessions altogether and our circumstances are extremely poor, we may not have the wherewithal for spiritual practise. However, the faults arising from being attached to them are many indeed. Just as if we spread honey on the edge of a sharp knife and then lick it, the pleasure of tasting its sweetness will be nothing compared with the pain of cutting our tongue. Our attachment to people and things is just like this. There is some fleeting pleasure to be had, but along with this, much suffering. Nagarjuna said that when we have an itchy rash on our skin, although there is some pleasure to be had from scratching it, there would be even more pleasure in not having the rash to start with. Similarly, when we are attached to people and things we may gain some pleasure; but we gain far greater happiness by having no attachments from the beginning.

(2) Methods for overcoming distractions directly

The antidote to a distracted mind is to produce meditative concentration. There are three levels of meditative concentration:

(i)   meditative concentration in common with the worldly;
(ii) meditative concentration in common with Hinayana; and
(iii) uncommon Mahayana meditative concentration.

(i) Meditative concentration in common with the worldly

With regard to worldly meditative concentration, there is a preparatory or preliminary stage followed by four actual states of form-realm meditative concentration and four actual states of formless-realm meditative concentration. The practitioner should train in these as much as possible. One who is serious about attaining enlightenment and practising to do so must first engage in these meditative absorptions common to the worldly.

(ii) Meditative concentration in common with Hinayana

The second meditative concentration is that held in common with the Shravakayana. On the shravaka path, one first contemplates the faults of the world, such as impermanence and suffering. The way to engage in the path common to the shravakas has two divisions: preparatory meditation and actual meditation.

The first, preparatory meditation, depends on the individual. If desirous attachment predominates, one should first meditate on ugliness. If discursive thought predominates, one should begin by concentrating on exhaling and inhaling, counting each inhalation and exhalation as one.

The second part, the actual meditation, involves meditating on the 'thirty-seven factors conducive to enlightenment' on the five paths, as follows: the 'four strongly placed mindfulnesses' are cultivated during the path of accumulation; the 'four correct endeavours' are practised during the 'level of heat,' the first part of the path of joining; the 'four legs of miracles' are practised on the second stage of the path of joining; the 'five spiritual faculties' are practised during the 'level of patience,' the third level of the path of joining; the 'five powers' are practised during the 'highest worldly dharma.' the 'eight branches of the aryas' path' (or eightfold noble path) are practised on the path of seeing; and the 'seven branches or limbs of enlightenment' are practised on the path of meditation. This is a general overview, which does not differentiate among the paths of shravakas, pratyekabuddhas and the Mahayana. It is said there are differences between the Hinayana and Mahayana with regard to the object, the subject, the aspect and the order of meditating on the 'thirty-seven factors conducive to enlightenment,' but the Hinayanist practice belongs to the Hinayana and so is omitted here.

The 'five spiritual faculties' refers to the faculty of faith, the faculty of enthusiasm or effort, the faculty of mindfulness, the faculty of concentration and the faculty of wisdom. The general characteristic of the five powers is the same as that of the five spiritual faculties, but they are called the five powers because they cannot be overpowered by their opposing factors. According to Mahayana, the order of the previously mentioned two is reversed; the 'seven branches of enlightenment' are practised on the path of seeing and the 'eight branches of arya's path' (or eightfold noble path) are practised on the path of meditation.

(iii) Uncommon Mahayana meditative concentration

Within the uncommon Mahayana, two systems are taught: the Mind-Only (or Cittamatrin) system, taught according to the explanation given by the great Indian teacher Arya Asanga in the *Compendium of Yanas*, and the Middle Way tradition, taught by Nagarjuna, Aryadeva and later by Shantideva. The following explanation is according to the instructions to be found in the *Bodhicharyavatara*, by Arya Shantideva.

Meditative concentration according to Middle Way school

According to the Middle Way school, as explained in the *Bodhicharyavatara*, the Mahayana method is to meditate directly on the enlightenment thought. However, in order to produce the enlightenment thought properly, it is necessary first to meditate on loving-kindness and compassion. Although it is not taught in the *Bodhicharyavatara* that one meditates on loving-kindness and compassion first, it is necessary to do so in order to produce the enlightenment thought.

(1) Meditating on loving-kindness

There are three kinds of objects of our meditation on loving-kindness: sentient beings who possess neither happiness nor suffering (in other words, who are in a neutral state); those who have not met the noble Dharma (the cause of happiness); and those who, despite having met the Dharma, have not yet attained the qualities of bodhisattvas and buddhas. With regard to the procedure for cultivating loving-kindness, we should first meditate on loving-kindness towards our parents and relatives. After having cultivated loving-kindness towards them, we should practise loving-kindness towards our enemies. Then we should cultivate that same benevolent mind towards all sentient beings. The characteristic of loving-kindness is to make the wish, 'May all beings have happiness and the causes of happiness.' This refers to happiness free from all defilements and all nonvirtues. To have the causes of happiness means not to engage in nonvirtuous deeds, which are the causes of unhappiness. In addition, we wish them great happiness and great virtue, which includes the wish that all their deeds be performed through the Mahayana motivation of working for the sake of sentient beings. Initially we should use words to try to generate this state of mind. It will not actually arise when we first begin, but if we accustom the mind to the concept of generating loving-kindness by constant heartfelt repetition of the words, real loving-kindness will eventually arise. Not only must we wish for all beings to be in a happy state and to have the causes of that happy state, but we must also make the resolve again and again: 'I must place all sentient beings in the state of happiness and the cause of happiness.'

Buddha himself said that the benefits arising from meditating on loving-kindness are immense. Even if we were to fill many universes with jewels and offer them to all the enlightened beings, the merit from this would not match the merits accrued during only a moment's meditation on loving-kindness. Therefore generating loving-kindness bestows immeasurable merit and inconceivable benefits upon ourselves and others.

(2) Meditating on compassion

To meditate on compassion, we first need to know who should be the objects of our meditation on compassion. According to a teaching by Maitreya (in the *Mahayanasutralamkara*), there are ten types of beings:

1. Beings who possess strong desire for beautiful forms, sounds and smells—the five objects of desire.
2. Beings obstructed from engaging in spiritual deeds by enemies, such as maras and so on.
3. Sentient beings of the three lower realms.
4. Those who perform nonvirtues continuously, such as butchers.
5. Those who have embarked on the path which is difficult to travel. This refers to sentient beings who, according to Cittamatra teachings, will never be liberated from cyclic existence.

6. Those who possess great fetters which bind them to samsara. This refers to the non-Buddhist Indian sectarians.

7. Those who have attachment to the form- and formless-realm meditative absorption, which is like being attached to great food mixed with poison. If one consumes such food, one will have a short period of pleasure, but soon afterwards one will suffer and die.

8. Those Hindu practitioners who involve themselves in austerities such as jumping from rocks, jumping into water, entering fires and so forth.

9. The Hinayana practitioners, not because they are on the wrong path but because they are on the longer path. Even though the paths of shravakas and pratyekabuddhas are causes for Buddhahood, because theirs is the 'crooked' way, they are also objects of Mahayana compassion.

10. Beginner bodhisattvas just embarking on the spiritual path, who have not yet cultivated enough merit or produced correct wisdom.

Maitreya also explained another way to categorize the objects of the meditation on compassion; that is, in terms of the six classes of people who engage in conduct opposite to the practice of the six perfections. According to this system, the objects of compassion are: those who are miserly; those who break their vows of morality; those who are short-tempered; those who are lazy; those who have distracted minds and those who are strongly attached to wrong views.

Shri Maitreya taught that the objects of our meditation on compassion may be divided broadly into two groups. The first consists of those who are in cyclic existence, and the second consists of those who strive to gain personal liberation and have fallen into the extreme of nirvana. The first group has two divisions:

(1) sentient beings who engage in the causes of suffering; and
(2) sentient beings who are experiencing the resultant suffering.

(1) Sentient beings who engage in the causes of suffering
This includes those who consistently commit nonvirtuous deeds in order to collect wealth or to gain personal happiness in this life. By

acting in such an improper manner, they accumulate the causes for further suffering. They will definitely face sufferings in the lower realms during future lives.

(2) Sentient beings who are experiencing the resultant suffering

This includes beings in the lower realms and even those who are experiencing suffering in the higher realms, such as human beings who live in poverty, who have diseases or mental distress, who are separated from relatives and loved ones, who have encountered enemies, who are aging, who live in fear or who are despised by those of higher status. Bodhisattvas also take beings in the second broad grouping (who strive to gain personal liberation and who have fallen into the extreme of nirvana) as objects of compassion, since they will have great difficulty in attaining the state of full and perfect enlightenment. This is because they have followed the path of the delaying diversion and it will therefore take forty great aeons longer for them to attain complete enlightenment than ordinary beings who engage in the Mahayana path from the beginning.

With regard to the method for generating compassion, compassion arises as a result of seeing suffering and reflecting upon it. If we visualize others in a state of suffering again and again and meditate on it, we will develop compassion. We should examine the condition of other beings carefully, and see the extent to which they have fallen into the three different types of suffering: the suffering of suffering, the suffering of change and the suffering of all conditioned existence, which pervades all cyclic existence. In addition, we should rely on a spiritual teacher to give us teachings about the methods for arousing compassion. When we see the various states of suffering, meditate on them and receive as many teachings as we can from our spiritual friend, it will be easier for us to generate compassion appropriately. One who has already generated compassion, either in a previous life or in this lifetime, will find it quite easy to generate compassion again now.

The method for meditating on compassion is first to focus on someone you love very much, such as your mother, your child or someone else very close to you. Then, using this person as your object of meditation, produce a feeling of compassion. It is necessary to use someone close and dear to you, because it is easier to produce compassion when you think of someone who brings you happiness.

If you begin by trying to practise compassion towards your enemies, you may experience revulsion instead, and the mind will become an infertile ground for producing compassion towards them now and in the future. Compassion may be defined as the mental state which wishes the other being or beings to be free from suffering and its causes. The 'causes of suffering' are emotional defilements and nonvirtuous deeds, which originate from clinging to 'I' and viewing it as real. With this understanding, we should make the compassionate aspiration, 'May all sentient beings be free from suffering and its causes, especially clinging to the "I," the root cause of all suffering.'

With regard to the benefits of practising compassion, it is stated in the *Arya Dharmasamgiti Sutra* (Compendium of Doctrine Sutra) that Arya Avalokiteshvara addressed Shakyamuni Buddha in the following terms. 'Blessed one, a bodhisattva need not train in many practices. If the bodhisattva has realized and adhered to one practice, then all Buddha's qualities will be in the palm of his hand. What is that one practice? The great compassion.' That is why all the temporary and ultimate benefits of Mahayana practices arise from compassion. It is also explained in the following way in the *Madhyamakavatara* (Entering the Middle Way). In the beginning, compassion leads to the altruistic practices of the Mahayana. In the middle, when one is training on the paths, compassion protects practitioners from falling into the Hinayana path. Finally, after accomplishing complete Buddhahood, it is through compassion that Buddha continues his activities to benefit sentient beings.

(3) Meditation on the enlightenment thought

Next we meditate on the enlightenment thought. There are two ways to meditate on the enlightenment thought:

    (i)   sameness of self and others; and
    (ii) exchanging self for others.

(i) Sameness of self and others

With regard to meditating on the sameness of self and others as it is taught in the *Bodhicharyavatara*, one should initially strive diligently to cultivate the equality of self and others, by thinking, 'All sentient beings are equal in wanting happiness and not wanting sufferings. I should protect other sentient beings as I would protect myself.' We should also resolve: 'I myself will bestow happiness on all living beings' and 'I myself will free sentient beings from suffering.' When any happiness comes to us, we should wish, 'May all sentient beings attain the same kind of happiness I am experiencing now.' Whenever we experience suffering we should wish, 'May all sentient beings be free from the kind of suffering I am experiencing now.' In this way we can equate ourselves with other beings. We should meditate again and again on the equality of self and others until it becomes a firm conviction. Once our mind becomes accustomed to the thought of equating ourselves with others, we can begin to meditate on exchanging self for others.

(ii) Exchanging self for others
There are two ways to meditate on exchanging self for others:

    (a)   the extensive method; and
    (b)   the brief method.

(a) The extensive method of exchanging self for others
When we come across someone who is our superior, we often become jealous. We imagine that he mistreats us, lacks compassion for us and looks down on us; that he criticizes us and blames us when things go wrong. We feel competitive towards those on the same level and try to prevent them from surpassing us. We look down on those at a lower level, thinking that they need not be treated as equals. In such ways we generate feelings of jealousy, competitiveness and pride towards those who are above us, on the same level or below us, respectively. In order to practise the meditation of exchanging self for others, we have to alter the way we think about these three categories of people. With respect to those who evoke our jealousy, the method to overcome it is to imagine exchanging our position with the other person's, placing ourselves in the high position and the other below us. Then we practise arousing jealousy towards this other person, who is actually us. When we see the negative consequences of this, we will give up the idea and stop feeling jealous of that person. Likewise, to cultivate the meditation on competitiveness towards those of equal status, we visualize ourselves in their place and visualize the enemy of equal status in

ours. Then we visualize the enemy, who is now in our place, competing against us in every possible way. After completing this meditation, we should think, 'If I experience such suffering merely through visualizing myself as the enemy of equal status competing with the enemy, now in my place, how can it be acceptable for me to compete against others?' In this way our competitive mind will pacify itself. One should apply the same process to pride. Generally we feel pride towards people of inferior status, inferior race, lower morality, lower practices, inferior physical form, lower economic position and so forth. In this visualization, we put the person of lower status in our own place. Then we visualize him generating pride towards us. He now becomes conceited about his excellent qualities compared with us, now in the lower status. After completing the meditation, we should think, 'If I experience such sufferings merely by meditating that others act in a conceited way towards me, how dare I ever feel conceited towards others?' In this way our mind will pacify conceit towards those of lower status.

The entire method of exchanging self for others with these three sets of people is explained in detail in the eighth chapter of the *Bodhicharyavatara*.

(b) The brief method of exchanging self for others

The short method for exchanging self for others is to visualize that we give our happiness and virtue to all living beings and take upon ourselves all the suffering, nonvirtue and unhappiness experienced by others. We think, 'May all my happiness and virtue ripen upon others' and 'May all the suffering, unhappiness and nonvirtue of others ripen upon me.' This is one way of practising the exchanging enlightenment thought. Nagarjuna stated that if we could give form to the merit arising by simply thinking, just for one moment, about exchanging self for others, it would be vaster than the skies of all three realms of existence. The method for accomplishing this meditation on the exchanging enlightenment thought is to meditate again and again on this thought in order to gain the state of full and complete enlightenment. After meditating again and again on this thought of exchanging ourselves with others, we will be able to accomplish the real meditation on the enlightenment thought. To achieve this, it is necessary to see the disadvantages of working only for our own benefit and to understand the great benefit of working for others.

In order to stabilize this enlightenment thought, we must examine very carefully the real purpose and benefit behind it. Then we will understand that we have been working solely for our own benefit for many lifetimes, never thinking of benefiting other sentient beings. This has led to the sufferings we are experiencing now. As long as we continue to seek only our own happiness, we will never gain the happiness we have always wanted. Instead we will gain only more and more suffering. When we understand that only through working for the benefit of others can we gain real happiness, we will appreciate the purpose of developing the enlightenment thought.

We should constantly examine our state of mind. In other words, we should develop introspection, like an inner spy, to monitor what we are doing. When we discover that we are keeping something that could be beneficial to others, we should relinquish it and give it to them. If jealousy arises, we should overcome it. For example, when we find ourselves thinking that someone else has greater happiness than we do, we should turn this jealousy against ourselves instead, by thinking, 'I am too happy. I have too much happiness in comparison with others. I am superior to others in happiness.' This creates a state of jealousy towards our own superiority and our own happiness instead of towards others. Furthermore, we should ask ourselves whether the deeds we perform through the three doors of actions are leading us to the lower realms, or whether we may be heading along the wrong path. If someone harms us, we should not regard this as harm caused by another. Instead we should understand that the suffering we are experiencing is due to our own karma. When we are acting against others, we should tell ourselves, 'I am now doing something against others.' Then we should think, 'I am now doing something wrong.' We need to examine very carefully what we are doing and state aloud to ourselves or to others that we have made a mistake, so we can halt the process. If people praise us, even if we think the praise is justified, we should not develop pride about the positive qualities they attribute to us. Instead we should mentally transfer these qualities to others and take on their qualities, even though they may seem inferior to ours. We should look on our good qualities as really belonging to other people and their lesser qualities as belonging to us. Furthermore, we should remember that whatever special qualities we may have, they are not permanent, and therefore it is pointless to become proud of them.

In brief, it is obvious that all our suffering is due to trying to gain happiness and benefit for ourselves alone and that we have been acting this way due to our self-cherishing. Our only benefit has been to take birth after birth within the six realms. If we really wish to break this cycle and strive to attain Buddhahood, the sole method is to work for others' benefit. To do this, we need to put aside our self-cherishing and begin to cherish others.

The Tibetan word for 'meditation' means 'habituation.' It means to habituate or accustom the mind to a certain spiritual mental state. For example, compassion arises effortlessly in the minds of bodhisattvas because they have become habituated to it. Furthermore, Buddha said that if we take just one verse of his teachings and study it, contemplate it and meditate on it, we will fully master the meaning of the teachings. In order to accomplish the perfection of meditative concentration, we must associate it with the four positive qualities and abandon the seven attachments to it.

With regard to the temporary benefits of meditative concentration, there are benefits which will accrue in this lifetime and benefits which will accrue in future lifetimes. The benefits which will accrue in this lifetime are as follows:

(1) One-pointed concentration (or calm abiding) will arise.
(2) Although the defilements are not yet uprooted, the manifested defilements of desire, anger and ignorance can be suppressed.
(3) The mind's agitation is pacified.
(4) We can equalize the eight worldly dharmas; that is, thoughts of happiness or sadness, gain or loss, etc. We will never again have any thoughts of wanting the four positive worldly dharmas at the expense of other people. For example, most of us usually hope to gain the four positive worldly dharmas or fear to encounter the four negative ones. All these hopes and fears will be neutralized through the accomplishment of meditative concentration; we will not be swayed to extremes, and the mind will remain in a state of equanimity.

(5) We will achieve physical and mental pliancy.
(6) We will attain various magical powers, such as flying through the sky, supernatural kinds of knowledge such as reading others' minds and states of higher consciousness.
(7) We will become pleasing to people and gods.

Due to accomplishing meditative concentration in this lifetime, there will be the following benefits in future lifetimes:

(1) our body, voice and mind will become suited to performing virtuous deeds; and
(2) we will easily attain the four meditative absorptions and the five kinds of clairvoyance, etc.

With regard to the ultimate benefits, when one attains complete Buddhahood, one will attain the four thorough purities to perform activities for the benefit of self and others:

(1) Thorough purity of body or basis means that the fully enlightened Buddha is able to take birth, remain or depart from worldly existence, as he wishes.
(2) Thorough purity of object means that the Buddha can accomplish miraculous powers or feats in order to benefit others, as in the examples of his manifesting miraculous emanations of nonexistent things and causing existing things to disappear miraculously.
(3) Thorough purity of enlightened thought means that the Buddha exercises dominion over all states of meditative absorption.
(4) Thorough purity of transcendental wisdom means that the Buddha exercises dominion over transcendental wisdom because he has severed the continuum of ignorance.

9

The Perfection of Wisdom

The sixth perfection is the perfection of wisdom. Wisdom is defined as the correct realization of the real nature of phenomena. This realization becomes the actual perfection of wisdom when it is conjoined with the preparation (enlightenment thought) and the conclusion (dedication). The opposing force to wisdom is wrong understanding. Those who are not on the Buddhist path do not have the proper means to gain an understanding of the ultimate nature of phenomena. Although those who belong to other religions and philosophies have a method for gaining wisdom, it is the wrong method. It does not comprehend the real state of things. With regard to those who follow the lower paths of the Buddhist tradition, such as the Hinayana, though they have methods for gaining wisdom, they do not have the methods which become the cause of Buddhahood. Therefore their wisdom is a limited or lesser form of wisdom.

The unfavourable result of lacking wisdom during this life is that we will always experience problems. We won't understand what to do and what to avoid doing. Those who possess wisdom understand the nature of reality, whereas those who lack wisdom cannot understand the nature of reality, any more than a wolf can sit in the place of a lion. If we lack wisdom, we won't develop a steady mind. Instead our mind will be timid and won't be of benefit either to ourselves or to others. Not only will we be unable to understand the scriptures, we will also not even possess worldly understanding. We will have no means by which to judge which actions to undertake and which to avoid. One who lacks wisdom will not be able to make progress on the path of Dharma. Just as a sick person cannot function properly, a person who lacks wisdom will not be able to undertake the practices properly and accomplish them. For example, if we attempt to meditate without an understanding of the Doctrine, we will not be able to accomplish the purpose of the meditation.

In the *Abhidharmakosha* (Treasury of Knowledge) the great Vasubhandu stated that without wisdom, one cannot pacify the afflictions which keep sentient beings wandering in the ocean of samsara. If we lack wisdom, therefore, we will not be able to discriminate between deeds to be adopted and deeds to be abandoned, and consequently we will be unable to perform virtuous actions. Regardless of where we are reborn, we will have inferior faculties. Due to our dull faculties, even if we practice, it will be the wrong practice; if we meditate, we will be unable to uproot self-grasping. Even if we do manage to diminish self-grasping, we will only be able to enter the cessation of the shravakas or pratyekabuddhas. Therefore possessing wrong understanding brings about many disadvantages, not only during the present lifetime but also in the future.

Wrong understanding is the opposing force to wisdom. There are two ways to overcome it:

(1) by countering its cause; or
(2) by countering it directly.

(1) Countering the cause of wrong understanding

The cause of wrong understanding is ignorance. The method for overcoming ignorance is first of all to study the Doctrine and then to contemplate on it. The contributing condition to wrong understanding is relying on a bad teacher or spiritual friend. To prevent this possibility, we should find an authentic teacher who understands the Doctrine well. Once we have met a teacher, we should examine him to ensure that he possesses both wisdom and proper conduct. If we find a teacher who has both of these qualities, he can then be relied upon. However, even if the teacher has good morality, unless he understands the meaning of the Dharma, he cannot help us overcome our ignorance. Therefore we need a teacher who not only has good morality but who also understands the true meaning of the Doctrine. Thus the way to overcome ignorance is to study and contemplate under the guidance of a good teacher. If we want to do anything properly, we must first understand the method. For instance, if we want to learn how to operate a computer, first we need to study the instructions. The same applies to Dharma. In order to practise Dharma and gain the proper result, we must first understand the teachings. Therefore understanding the Doctrine is the essential basis for our practice.

(2) Directly countering the resultant wrong understanding

The direct method for overcoming the resultant wrong understanding is to produce and further develop correct understanding. First of all we must be able to distinguish between mistaken understanding and correct understanding. Then we must refute the former and establish the latter. With regard to refuting mistaken understandings, there are two divisions:

(i) refuting mistaken understandings of the non-Buddhist Indian schools; and

(ii) refuting mistaken understandings of other Buddhist schools.

(i) Refuting mistaken understandings of the non-Buddhist Indian schools

(a) Presenting their views

Although there are many non-Buddhist Indian schools, they may be broadly classified into two categories: those who expound eternalism and those who expound nihilism. Eternalism is the view of an inherently and permanently existing self, which remains even after liberation is attained. When that permanent self is bound by karma and afflictions, it is said to be in samsara; when that self frees itself from karma and afflictions, that permanent self is regarded as having been liberated. Nihilism is the view that the self exists inherently while the sentient being is alive but then ceases at death. In other words, nihilists accept only this life. The nihilists also claim that there is no logic apart from what is perceived. In other words, whatever is seen in this life exists, and whatever is not seen does not exist. They do not accept a continuation of cyclic existence after death, nor do they accept the liberation of nirvana.

(b) Refuting their views

By simply cutting through the view of the self of person and the self of phenomena, one can understand that all phenomena lack inherent existence. Hence one is freed from both views. As said in *Madhyamakavatara*, there is a difference between the person and the 'self of person.' The 'self of person' signifies the inherent or substantial person. There is also a difference between a cognizable thing and the 'self of a cognizable thing.' The mere 'cognizable thing' refers to form, sound and the other objects of sensory and mental perception. The 'self of a cognizable thing' refers to its inherent existence. The view that phenomena exist inherently is refuted by the analytical reasoning of non-arising from the four extremes,[4] and the view of self of person is refuted through the analysis of the five modes.[5] If one attains an intellectual understanding of the nonexistence of the self of person and the self of phenomena through applying these two sets of reasonings, one can overcome wrong speculative views of nihilism and eternalism.

(ii) Refuting the mistaken understandings of other Buddhist sects

The Buddhist tradition is subdivided into two principal schools: Mahayana and Hinayana. The wisdom expounded by both schools is faultless. However, after the passing away of Buddha, various schools of thought developed. Many of these schools introduced erroneous

---

4   The analytical reasoning of the four extremes is set out in detail in the *Madhyamakavatara* by Chandrakirti, which is available in several English translations. This reasoning demonstrates that things do not arise from themselves, from others, from both self and others or without a cause.

5   The analysis of the five modes uses the chariot as the basis of analogy to demonstrate the nonexistence of a personal self in the following way: (1) there is no chariot which is other than its parts; (2) there is no chariot which is the same as its parts; (3) there is no chariot which inherently possesses its parts; (4) there is no chariot which inherently depends on its parts; (5) there is no chariot on which its parts inherently depend. In the same way, when we look for an inherent self, we will not find it. Acharya Chandrakirti later added the following two additional points: (6) there is no chariot which is the mere collection of its parts; and (7) there is no chariot which is the shape of its parts. This expanded analysis is known as the seven point (or mode) reasoning of the chariot.

teachings on the views. The fundamental difference between the non-Buddhist Hindu sects and the Buddhist sects is that, whereas the non-Buddhist Hindu sects have other teachers, the various Buddhist sects derive from differing interpretations of the Buddha's teachings.

The topic on refuting the mistaken understandings of other Buddhist sects has three divisions:

(a) refuting the Hinayana tenets;
(b) refuting the contention that provisional Mahayana schools are definitive; and
(c) refuting the acceptance of teachings which are neither Hinayana nor Mahayana as the Buddha's teachings.

(a) Refuting the Hinayana tenets

There are two Indian Hinayana philosophical schools: Vaibashika and Sautrantika. Both claim that the mind is truly existent, and although they do not accept the true existence of gross form, they regard the tiniest, indivisible atoms as truly existent. They maintain that there is a 'truly existent momentary consciousness' which cannot be divided by time. There are no differences between these two schools with respect to accepting consciousness, but there are differences with regard to the characteristic nature of atoms. These schools accept only the Hinayana teachings; they do not regard the Mahayana scriptures as the teachings of the Buddha.

(b) Refuting the contention that provisional Mahayana schools are definitive

With regard to the schools which uphold the Mahayana tenets, there are two: the Cittamatra school and the Madhyamika school. Cittamatrins do not maintain that objects—that is, form, sound, smell, taste, touch or the perception which grasps them—are truly existent. However, they maintain that the mere clarity of the mind is truly existent. Within the Cittamatra school, there are two principal sub-schools: True Aspect Cittamatra and False Aspect Cittamatra. The former sub-school asserts that dualistic mental images are truly existent, but the separately projected external objects are not. False Aspect Cittamatrins do not assert that even the mental images of the objective and subjective mind are inherently existent.

There is no difference between the Cittamatra schools and the Madhyamika school regarding the presentation of the method of practice or the conduct; the difference lies only in the view. Unlike the Cittamatra school, the Madhyamika school does not accept any phenomena as truly existent. The Madhyamika school also has two principal sub-schools: Svatantrika and Prasangika. According to Sakya scholars, there are no differences in view between these two schools. The only difference lies in the procedure used for establishing the ultimate nature of phenomena through analytical reasoning. Sakya Pandita maintains that even the Buddhist philosophical tenets claiming to be Madhyamaka must be refuted if they fall into the extremes of eternalism and nihilism. For detailed refutations, one should consult his *Treasure of Reasoning (rigs pa'i gter)* and *Distinctions Between the Tenets (grub pa'i mtha'i dbye ba)*.

(c) Refuting the teachings which are neither Hinayana nor Mahayana as being the Buddha's teachings

Four Buddhist schools, all of which arose in Tibet, expound mistaken views concerning the Doctrine. These are:

(1) the system of the Chinese master Hö-shang Mahayana;
(2) the later generation approach which follows the Chinese system;
(3) the approach widely known today, which asserts the False Aspect Cittamatrin meditation as mahamudra; and
(4) a school which arose out of the Madhyamaka, expounding the specious perfection of wisdom as mahamudra.

(1) The system of the Chinese Master Hö-shang Mahayana

At the time of King Trisong Deutsen,[6] a Chinese master known as Hö-shang Mahayana was giving Buddhist teachings in Tibet. He taught that there was no need to study the Doctrine or to perform any of the preliminary practices, such as prostrations, circumambulation or meditation on loving-kindness and compassion. According to his teaching, all we need do to attain the state of Buddhahood is to meditate on emptiness directly. He claimed that just by meditating on emptiness we can realize the nature of the

---

6   Khri srong lde'u bstan (742–797)

mind. He called this the 'singly efficacious white remedy,' by means of which we will be able to overcome all obstacles and attain the state of Buddhahood, without studying or undertaking the method practices. There were five commentaries written by him and by others on this teaching, and it spread widely throughout Tibet. It was even said to have reached other parts of Central Asia.

Hö-shang Mahayana's method for meditating on emptiness was to sit with a blank mind, without thinking about anything. It was presented as just a matter of resting the mind without creating any thoughts at all. He maintained that since both virtuous thoughts and nonvirtuous thoughts bind us to cyclic existence, virtuous thoughts are of no benefit. When King Trisong Deutsen heard about this form of meditation, he realized that it differed considerably from the teachings he had received earlier from Indian masters. So he asked Yeshe Wangpo (one of the disciples of Shantarakshita, the great master from India who brought Buddhist teachings to Tibet) his opinion about the method of solely meditating on emptiness as a means of attaining Buddhahood. Yeshe Wangpo advised the king to follow the instructions of Acharya Shantarakshita. He explained that Acharya Shantarakshita had prophesied that although the heretical approach would not take root in Tibet, because Guru Padmasambhava had entrusted Tibet to the care of the twelve 'tenma' goddesses, two different systems of teaching would develop. He explained, 'In the same way that there is no day without night, no right without left, no waxing moon without waning moon, it is the nature of interdependence for both pure and impure teachings to arise. Since delighting in emptiness is a degeneration of the view (one of the five degenerations taught by Lord Buddha in a sutra), it is natural that delight would be taken in emptiness, not only by people in Tibet but by all the people in whom the five impurities thrive. If this teaching spreads, it will harm the Doctrine of the Buddha in general. In his testament, Shantarakshita also advised that you should invite his disciple, Kamalashila, to Tibet to debate with the Chinese master. The system advocated by the winner should be followed.'

On hearing this, the king sent for Kamalashila, and a debate was formally arranged between the two masters. The king declared that the teachings of the winner would prevail and the teachings of the loser would be banned. The winner's teachings would be established as the correct teachings, hence forward to be followed throughout

Tibet. Both agreed to these terms, and the debate began. First of all, Kamalashila asked Hö-shang to present his theories. Hö-shang put forth his position, maintaining that any kind of action, whether virtue or nonvirtue, will result only in birth within samsara. Therefore, he concluded, one must discard the cause of samsaric birth, which means one must avoid carrying out any action of body, speech or mind. For example, just as a cloud obscures the sun regardless of whether it is white or black, likewise any kind of action, whether virtuous or nonvirtuous, will lead to rebirth in samsara. Therefore one should meditate on the nonconceptual state right from the beginning of one's practice, and there is no need to meditate on compassion and loving-kindness or to practise giving, morality or patience. The only way to enlightenment, he explained, was to stop the flow of conceptual thoughts entirely. He likened his approach to an eagle swooping down from the sky and alighting on a treetop. According to him, the approach advocated by Kamalashila was a very slow one. It was analogous to a monkey climbing up the trunk of a tree from the ground and eventually arriving at the top. Even though both the eagle and the monkey will reach the top of the tree, it will take the monkey far longer. He said that Kamalashila's approach was inferior because it started from the bottom and had to develop stage by stage. In this way, he claimed, Kamalashila's teachings were inferior to his own.

Kamalashila asked Hö-shang whether the eagle which descended from the sky had been born in a nest or on a rock and then developed, grew wings and gradually learned to fly, or whether it had been born in the sky already equipped with strong body and wings. Hö-shang replied that there had never been a case in the world in which birds were born full-grown in the sky possessing a strong body and wings. We can see plainly, he said, that birds are born in a nest or a rock, and that they grow wings, develop strength and then fly away.

Kamalashila pointed out that as described, Hö-shang Mahayana's teaching did not differ from his own. His method also began from a low position and then developed stage by stage, just as the bird had to grow and develop stage by stage. It is said that Hö-shang was unable to respond to this. Again, Kamalashila argued that the method which involved stopping all thought and just leaving the mind resting in a state of non-thought was invalid. He inquired whether Hö-shang actually meant that one should stop only certain thoughts, or that one should stop all thoughts altogether. If he meant one should stop only certain thoughts, then someone who was sleeping would be in a state of meditation, because that person would be stopping certain thoughts by sleeping. But he believed that was not what Hö-shang had meant to say. On the other hand, if he meant to say that one must stop absolutely all thoughts, did he mean that the thought 'I want to meditate' had to be stopped, or that one would have to think, 'I want to meditate?' If one did not need to produce the thought, 'I want to meditate,' then all living beings who have never even thought about meditating must be in a state of meditation, because they also lack the thought of either wanting to meditate or not wanting to meditate. Alternatively, if one needs to have the thought, 'I must meditate,' then since this is an actual thought, it would contradict Hö-shang's teaching that we should have no thoughts at all. Thus Kamalashila defeated Hö-shang both by example and by philosophical argument.

It is said that once again, Hö-shang Mahayana did not respond. When the king asked him to give a reply, he could not. The king said he was so spellbound that he looked as though he had been struck by lightning. The king decided that the teaching brought by Hö-shang Mahayana from China would no longer be propagated in Tibet. Instead, he proclaimed that everybody in Tibet must henceforward embrace the teachings expounded by Nagarjuna and brought from India by Shantarakshita and others.

(b) The approach of the later generation, which follows the Chinese system

Later on there arose a school in Tibet which advocated theories similar to those of Hö-shang Mahayana. This school maintained that, although the mind must not be left in a totally blank state, it should rest in a 'non-artificial' or 'natural' state, which does not create any thoughts whatsoever. They termed this 'mahamudra.' This state was likened to a brahmin spinning his sacred thread. According to this school, there are seven faults of the mind: three delaying diversions and four lapses. By leaving the mind in the non-artificial, natural state that has abandoned these seven faults, one would be able to gain an understanding of the true nature of things. Sakya Pandita argues that this teaching is incorrect, first of all because the term 'mahamudra' cannot be used in this way. He points out that there are no teachings on mahamudra in the Sutra, Vinaya or Abhidharma scriptures. Mahamudra teachings are found only in the Vajrayana, where an explanation is included in the four divisions of Tantra. However, the method in question here is not the mahamudra explained in the four divisions of Tantra. This is because the explanations contained in the four divisions of Tantra do not advocate simply leaving the mind in a non-artificial state, without the proper basis. In fact, the particular methodology advocated by this Tibetan school has been described in the teachings as the 'meditative cultivation of delusion.' Sakya Pandita further maintains that comparing the naturalness of the unravelled mind with the brahmin spinning the sacred thread is not an appropriate analogy. This is so because when spinning, it is impossible to produce fine thread without altering the fibre by lifting it, drawing it out and twisting it, tightening it if loose, loosening it if tight, regulating the thickness, removing knotty bunches and so forth. By this stage the thread is by no means in a non-artificial state. In fact, if it were left in its unaltered state, it would remain nothing more than a pile of raw fibre. Furthermore, if one were to practise the so-called mahamudra of simply leaving the mind in an unaltered state, what need would there be for any religious instruction at all? Sakya Pandita also points out that the seven faults of the mind, which this school claimed must be overcome in order to gain the state of ultimate reality, are actually very minor faults. There are many far greater faults to be discarded before the mind can be placed in the state of ultimate reality. In this way he refuted the teachings of this school.

(3) The approach widely known today, which asserts the False Aspect Cittamatrin meditation as mahamudra

Another school claims that the teachings on mahamudra should be practised in four distinct stages. The first stage involves placing the mind in one-pointedness. The second stage is for the mind to go beyond all conditioned extremes, 'free from elaborations.' The third stage is known as 'one taste,' which means that everything, 'all dharmas,' have just one nature. The fourth stage is known as 'devoid of meditation' or 'no need for meditation.' Sakya Pandita mentions that during his time, some Tibetans applied these four kinds of False Aspect Cittamatrin meditations to the five paths and the ten bodhisattva stages, believing this to be the mahamudra meditation. They applied 'one-pointedness' to the first stage (the paths of accumulation and joining); 'free from elaborations' to the impure seven stages (path of seeing and first part of the path of meditation); 'one taste' to the three pure bodhisattva levels (eighth, ninth and tenth, the higher part of the path of meditation) and 'devoid of meditation' to complete Buddhahood.

Sakya Pandita maintains that this practice is invalid. This is because firstly, the four stages identified by this school are really the teachings of the Cittamatrin school, whereas mahamudra meditation is a Vajrayana system; and secondly, this system was not taught directly by Buddha. It is purely a creation by later practitioners in Tibet.

(4) The school which arose out of the Madhyamaka, expounding the specious perfection of wisdom as mahamudra

One school claiming to follow Madhyamaka teaches a method by which the mind is equated with space. Based on a line in the *Prajnaparamitasutra* which says, 'He set forth to sentient beings a teaching stating that all the factors of existence have the natural mode of space,' this school developed a system called the 'three introductions': introducing all factors of existence as mind, introducing the mind as space and introducing space as emptiness. Based on another quotation from the *Prajnaparamitasutra*, 'Absence of memory and absence of apprehension is the recollection of complete Buddhahood,' one school maintains that the absence of memory and apprehension itself constitutes mahamudra. Yet another school claims that by meditating on the luminosity of the mind, they are meditating on mahamudra. They base this on the quotation in the Sutra which says, 'That which is mind is the nonexistence of mind, for mind is by nature luminosity, luminously clear.'

Many such categories of 'mahamudra' are currently practised in Tibet. Sakya Pandita says that although some of the methods are valid, since they aspire to realize the Madhyamika teachings, they should not be called 'mahamudra' teachings, because they do not follow the mahamudra taught by Buddha. Their teachings involve misconceptions about what mahamudra actually is. He says that the adherents of this school can only attain a semblance of the perfection of discriminative understanding, since they are ignorant about how to cultivate it in meditation. Even if there are some who do know how to cultivate it, these meditations are not the mahamudra of the mantra tradition but merely meditations of the perfections class of teaching.

Basically, beginning with Hö-shang's school, all these four schools claim that the preliminaries to meditation are unnecessary, and that one can attain understanding of ultimate reality by meditating directly on emptiness alone. In other words, one could attain Buddhahood in this way, without doing any other practices. But Sakya Pandita refutes this assertion. He maintains that in order to attain Buddhahood, it is absolutely necessary not only to possess wisdom but also to develop method or skilful means, such as practising loving-kindness and compassion and so on. In fact, the teachings state quite clearly that both wisdom and skilful means are required in order to attain Buddhahood. If we possess only skilful means such as compassion, we cannot go beyond worldly existence. Conversely, if we possess only wisdom without skilful means, we will fall into a lower path, because this belongs to the Hinayana understanding of reality. Although it leads to a form of liberation, it is incomplete because it is not full and perfect enlightenment. Thus, in order to gain the state of Buddhahood, it is absolutely essential to cultivate both wisdom and method.

Some of the views outlined above are held to this day by certain sections of the Kagyud school, but not by the entire school. The Kagyud school became famous and influential in Tibet mainly on account of the Vajrayana teachings introduced to Tibet from India through the Kagyud lineage; its teachings on Paramitayana were less effective. With regard to the view of ultimate reality, the earlier Kagyud teachings were similar to those of Sakya. Their methods for realizing ultimate reality were said to be the most effective and the best of the various methods brought to Tibet. However, there have always been debates in Tibet amongst the different schools, and there are even people who disagree with the views Sakya Pandita espouses in *Clarifying the Sage's Intent*.

Meditating on emptiness without practising compassion is not a correct practice, because it is not a cause for full and perfect enlightenment. Even if one possesses great faith in the teachings, renounces worldly existence and meditates correctly on the selflessness of person, but does so without employing the method practices such as loving-kindness and great compassion, one will attain only the result of personal liberation. Hence it is apparent that the meditation on wisdom alone, although it may be a correct meditation, will not lead to enlightenment. In fact, if one practises meditative concentration with insight wisdom of a conventional nature and overcomes the gross defilements of the desire realm, this will lead to rebirth in the form realm. If one's meditation develops further and one abides in the realization that sees all phenomena as clear and empty like space, this will lead to rebirth in the 'sphere of infinite space,' the first of the four formless realms. If one abides in the realization that sees all phenomena as the nature of mind, this will lead to rebirth in the 'sphere of infinite consciousness,' the second formless realm. If one abides in the realization that sees nothingness, this will lead to rebirth in the 'sphere of nothingness,' the third formless realm. If one abides in the realization that sees all phenomena as neither existent nor nonexistent, this will lead to rebirth in the 'sphere of neither existence nor nonexistence,' the fourth formless realm. In short, cultivating such meditations on emptiness, without realizing the selflessness of person and the selflessness of phenomena, will lead to rebirth within the form or formless realms; it will not lead even to arhatship, let alone to Buddhahood. So even though these meditations may be extremely effective in certain ways, they are not a cause for liberating one from the realms of existence, because the results of these meditations fall within the three realms of cyclic existence.

There are so-called practitioners with merits inferior to those who meditate on the formless meditations, who have not yet discarded the desirous attachment of the form realm yet meditate on the inexpressible and think proudly, 'I have realized phenomena.' Such people are not devoted to the correct Doctrine and will be reborn as long-life gods, one of the eight 'restless states.' There are practitioners inferior even to those described above who, lacking understanding of the two selflessnesses and without having abandoned the desirous attachments of the desire realm, meditate on the inexpressible without any thoughts at all. They also will be reborn in one of the eight restless states[7] known as the barbarian or

---

7   The eight restless states are: (1) being born in the hell realms; (2) being

the mute fool. There are others who, during the meditation on emptiness, think that there is absolutely no difference between virtue and nonvirtue, since everything is in a state of emptiness and consequently neither virtue nor nonvirtue exist. As a result of this belief, they may commit many nonvirtuous deeds, despite the fact that they engage in meditation. If these people commit great nonvirtue, they will be reborn in the hells; if they commit a middling type of nonvirtue; they will be reborn in the hungry-ghost realm; and if they commit lesser nonvirtue, they will be reborn in the animal realm.

Correct Wisdom

In order to attain correct wisdom, there are three things we must accomplish:

(1) we must establish the correct view;
(2) we must meditate on that correct view; and
(3) we must complement the wisdom we have attained with our daily activities.

(1) Establishing the correct view

To establish the correct view, we must study the Buddha's Doctrine, especially the teachings which deal mainly with wisdom, such as the *Prajnaparamitasutras*. We should also study later teachings or commentaries, such as Nagarjuna's teachings on the Middle Way, Chandrakirti's *Madhyamakavatara*, and the ninth chapter of *Bodhicharyavatara* by Shantideva, which deals with wisdom. Buddha taught that it is necessary first to listen to the teachings and then to study them and contemplate on them, before we undertake the actual practice of meditation. Some of us may be tempted to undertake meditation practices without having properly studied and understood the teachings on wisdom. If we go ahead and do so, we may find ourselves meditating on something which was not taught

---

born as a hungry ghost; (3) being born as an animal; (4) being born as a long-life god; (5) being born amongst barbarians, who are ignorant of the teachings; (6) being born with wrong views, such as nihilism or eternalism; (7) being born at a time or place where Buddha has not appeared; and (8) being born as a deaf mute.

directly by the Buddha in the Sutras, nor expounded in the reliable commentaries composed later on. We may thereby fall into the wrong path. To do so would divert us from our main objective, full enlightenment.

Of course there are some people who don't believe there is any benefit to be obtained through studying the teachings. On the contrary, there is great benefit, because we cannot practise effectively unless we first develop our understanding through listening, studying and contemplating. If we comprehend the Doctrine well, we are unlikely to be misled into erroneous beliefs and practices. We will not fall off the path and we will be less likely to make mistakes. Studying is not an end in itself; the point is to enable us to understand the path to enlightenment and to follow it correctly.

Once upon a time there was a Buddha known as 'King Exalted Like Sumeru,' who had a bodhisattva disciple named Dharmabhanakacaryavisuddhi. After this Buddha passed away, his disciple continued to give teachings in the same way they had been presented by that Buddha. At that time, there also lived a monk by the name of Bikshu Caryamati, who was very learned in the teachings on morality, or Vinaya. Not only was he learned, but he was also a very good practitioner, and his general conduct was exemplary. Furthermore, he was extremely fond of meditation and preferred staying in quiet and isolated places where he practised his meditation in a highly disciplined manner. He had many disciples who also meditated in this way. For his own benefit and that of others, this monk constructed a temple in a remote location. He told his disciples that Buddha himself had taught about the necessity of meditating in isolated places. He even established a rule that none of his monks should leave the temple to teach.

The bodhisattva Dharmabhanakacaryavisuddhi happened to be staying at Bikshu Caryamati's temple at that time. Whenever Dharmabhanakacaryavisuddhi went to the town to give teachings, Bikshu Caryamati would be displeased. He would tell the bodhisattva again and again that he must not go to town, and that he should remain within the temple grounds. The bodhisattva did not listen to him. One day Caryamati warned him that if he went out again, he would be forbidden to live in the temple. For three months the bodhisattva refrained from visiting the town, remaining within the temple precincts as he had been instructed to do. However, the people who had grown accustomed to listening to his teachings became upset, because they had no one to teach them. Their minds began to stray, and they started to act improperly. Because of this, the bodhisattva decided to leave that isolated place and began to travel to other towns again to teach the people. When Caryamati heard about what the bodhisattva was doing, he became agitated. He had also heard that the bodhisattva's disciples were not acting in accordance with the Vinaya teachings. A lack of faith sprang up in his mind and he told many people, 'This monk is corrupt in his morality and lives in society.' Thus he obstructed the bodhisattva by criticizing him and his followers and by telling people not to attend his teachings. By doing this, he turned them away from listening to religious teachings.

After the monk Caryamati died, it is said that he was reborn in the Avici hell, and that he had to stay there for an extremely long time. For sixty lifetimes he heard unpleasant words spoken to him. In thirty-two thousand lives he fell from the ordained state (i.e., reverted from monastic to daily life). For many hundreds and thousands of lifetimes, his moral faculties were dull. Lord Buddha said: 'O son of noble family, at that time I myself was that monk Caryamati.' Through his practice of virtue at this time and also through greater practices, the bodhisattva in this story become Buddha Akshobya. The point here is that the negative consequences of obstructing the Buddha's teachings, especially the Mahayana teachings, are severe indeed. Therefore we must be very careful.

Once upon a time in China there was a very learned monk who always tried to obstruct others from giving Dharma teachings, because he thought he was special and that his teachings were superior by far. If others tried to teach, he would always interrupt them by criticizing what they said and trying to show that they did not know the Doctrine properly. He even composed a text entitled *The Exposition of Snakes,* which explained that other teachers lacked understanding of the Buddha's Doctrine and were thus akin to snakes. Because it was extremely well-written, this book became very popular and the teacher grew quite famous. One day when he was on his way home after chanting prayers, he fell from his horse. Then all at once his body started to transform itself into the body of a snake. When his disciples saw what was happening, they had no idea what to do. The learned monk told them that they should leave while his mind was still human, because when his mind changed into a snake's mind, he might try to harm them. By that time his body had become completely transformed into that of a snake, and he slid away into a nearby forest. The point of this story is that the negative consequences of trying to obstruct the Dharma can be so powerful that the result may ripen within one lifetime.

Buddha said that we should always offer prayers in order to benefit sentient beings. He said that all solemn resolutions are included within one resolution: 'May I uphold the noble teachings.' In other Sutras, it is stated that there is more merit in teaching one four-line verse to a sentient being than in filling the entire world with the seven kinds of precious substances and offering it to the Three Jewels. This is because offering wealth is the cause of excellent worldly benefits, but teaching Buddha's Doctrine is the cause for going beyond cyclic existence.

There are great benefits to be obtained by studying the holy Dharma, and it is a very great fault not to study it. Unless we acquire vast knowledge of the Doctrine, we cannot understand the two truths: relative truth and ultimate truth. Unless we understand the two truths, we cannot understand the meaning of the profound scriptures, and we will not be able to attain liberation. There are different interpretations and definitions of the two truths among the various Tibetan schools. Broadly speaking, relative truth may be defined as everything which appears to the mind deluded by ignorance, and ultimate truth may be defined as that which is seen by an undeluded mind. There are two types of relative truth: correct relative truth and incorrect relative truth. For example, someone who focuses his eyes on the moon sees the moon, and everyone else would also agree that the moon is there. This is known as correct relative truth. If a person affected by an eye disease looks at the sky and says that he sees two moons, this is an example of incorrect relative truth.

With regard to ultimate truth, there are two kinds: on the one hand there is the ultimate truth, which may be understood by ordinary people through proper examination and study, and on the other there is the ultimate truth seen directly by Hinayana aryas and by bodhisattvas and buddhas. The Dharma practices we do, such as the foundation practices, the actual practices and even the resultant attainment, are all within the realm of relative truth. Although the ultimate state of basis, path and result is included in ultimate truth, the practices and the results themselves are considered to be relative truth. The indivisibility of relative and ultimate truth is known as the 'nondifferentiation of the two truths.' Some people ask whether relative and ultimate truth are the same or different. We really cannot say. If we say they are the same, we face contradictions. If we say they are different, we also face contradictions. So we can never say either that they are the same or that they are different. For example, if we see a carp and say, 'it is ultimate reality,' we are claiming to see the ultimate truth when we are actually seeing only the relative form. That creates contradiction. Conversely, if we say that these two truths differ from each other when they are actually inseparable, we also contradict ourselves.

In order to meditate on ultimate truth, it is necessary first to listen to or study the teachings on emptiness or selflessness and also to contemplate on them. Then we must put them into our meditation. If we try to meditate on ultimate reality without a thorough understanding of the teachings, realization will not arise. If realization does not arise, we will not realize the ultimate nature of all phenomena. Unless we realize the ultimate nature of all phenomena, we will be unable to attain liberation. In order to understand ultimate reality, we must first of all carefully examine the self, which we call the 'I.' We can all accept that from the relative viewpoint, there is an appearance of this thing called 'I,' and it seems to function. However, when we analyse this 'I' carefully from the ultimate viewpoint, we will find that it has no reality of its own. There are various sets of logical reasonings which prove the nonexistence of the self at the ultimate level. The primary method involves investigating whether the self is the same as the five aggregates or differs from them. If we investigate carefully through the appropriate reasoning and meditation, we will conclude that this thing we call 'I' is neither the same as the five aggregates nor different from them. Since they are neither the same nor different, they have no reality of their own from the ultimate point of view. As we cannot even find them, we certainly cannot establish them to be either the same or different. When we cannot locate this 'I' which we continually grasp as truly existent, we will begin to lose our attachment to it. We will begin to realize the nonreality of this 'I' from the ultimate point of view. In this way we will be able to eliminate the notion of the self of person.

However, overcoming only the view of the self of person is not enough, because this is not the complete wisdom. Many other schools also accept the selflessness of person but regard outer phenomena such as aggregates as truly existent. However, through studying the Madhyamika teachings, we learn that not only is the self of person devoid of true existence, but all phenomena are likewise devoid of true existence. There are basically two steps to reaching this understanding: firstly, just as a person does not ultimately exist, one sees that all phenomena, such as aggregates and physical objects, lack reality; and secondly, having seen that all outer phenomena are the nature of mind, one examines to see whether the mind itself is real. We will see that the mind does not have any true identity of its own either. Thus we can establish that neither outer phenomena nor the mind exist inherently.

The Madhyamika school teaches that things are ultimately neither existent nor nonexistent; that they are neither empty nor non-empty. In other words, they are beyond conceptualisation. This means that when scrutinized properly, entities we normally consider to be truly existent, such as the self, the mind or external phenomena, are found to have no reality of their own. Since they were never truly there, it cannot be said that they are either existent or nonexistent. At the relative level we can say that a fruit is sweet or not sweet, sour or not sour. However, at the ultimate level, if we examine either ourselves or outer phenomena, we find that they have never existed, right from the beginning. There is no question, therefore, as to whether they are existent or nonexistent, empty or non-empty. Thus we can understand that the ultimate reality of phenomena is beyond conceptualisation.

These teachings on ultimate reality are taught in all four Tibetan schools. It cannot be said that one school is better than another, because they all propound the same teachings on ultimate reality, albeit using different methods. It is said that the meditational method of the Gelug school with regard to the view of ultimate reality is slightly different. However the actual teachings are basically the same. The other three Tibetan schools—Sakya, Kagyud and Nyingma—have the same methods for meditating on ultimate reality. There is one school known as 'emptiness devoid of other,' whose way of explaining ultimate reality is slightly different. However, its methods for meditating on ultimate reality do not differ from those of the other schools.

(2) Meditating on the correct view

Before we can meditate correctly on ultimate reality, it is necessary to establish the correct intellectual understanding of the view. For that reason, the teachings on the view are always presented before guiding the followers in meditation on the ultimate view. Before we begin the actual meditation, we must find a quiet place. We should sit on a comfortable seat and be at ease. Our body should be positioned in the correct meditation posture, neither too relaxed nor too rigid. Our eyes should be facing in front of us, not open too wide nor shut too tight, but half-open and relaxed. This is the correct physical posture for meditation. It is also very important to be careful about our breath. We should not try to produce any special kind of breathing, but just let the breath flow naturally.

First recite the uncommon refuge verses and the prayers of the enlightenment thought. Then, based on your ascertainment of selflessness gained through study and contemplation, meditate as well as you can on each of the two types of selflessness (the selflessness of person and the selflessness of phenomena) in turn. Once you have attained the meditation, you should try to keep your mind in that state for as long as possible. At the conclusion, dedicate the merits out of compassion to all sentient beings, especially to those who are unable to realize the ultimate reality of the person and phenomena and are thus roaming in the suffering world. In the off-session, after waking from the meditation, you should continue to see all things as illusory by nature, so that you do not grasp them as true. Just think that whatever you do, whatever teachings you give or listen to, it is all just magical illusion.

(3) Complementing the wisdom you have attained with daily activities

In order to perfect this realization, it is necessary to maintain proper conduct, because otherwise you will never achieve proper meditation or correct wisdom. If you listen to the teachings, study them and contemplate on them while maintaining pure morality, you will be able to accomplish the three higher trainings: the higher training in morality, the higher training in meditation and the higher training in wisdom. According to certain teachings, another method involves practising the *Sevenfold Prayer*, which is found in the *Bodhicharyavatara* and in the *Prayer of Samantabhadra*. This prayer includes seven kinds of virtuous actions for accumulating merit. One should recite the *Sevenfold Prayer* three times during the day and three times at night, in conjunction with the rituals of taking refuge, the aspiring enlightenment thought and the engaging enlightenment thought. It is said that by doing these ten Dharma practices together, one will be able to perfect the realization quickly and easily. In order for your practice of wisdom to become the perfection of wisdom, it must be associated with the four qualities and not be polluted by the seven attachments, which were detailed in the chapters on the earlier perfections.

The benefits arising from wisdom

By practising the perfection of wisdom, we will gain many benefits. During the present lifetime, we will acquire knowledge of worldly phenomena, attaining a degree of scholarship and fame. People will believe what we say, and we will be able to help them because of their faith in us. We will also be able to overcome all of this life's fears. In our future lifetimes, we will be able to enhance our wisdom by making it vast and pure; we will be endowed with acute moral faculties and a sharp intellect; we will be able to see buddhas and bodhisattvas directly; and we will be able to hear many teachings and also to teach many aspects of the doctrine. With regard to the ultimate benefits, when we gain the state of Buddhahood, we will understand phenomena exactly as they are and in their full extent; we will acquire the confidence of the four special kinds of knowledge known as the four individually correct cognitions; we will acquire the four kinds of fearlessness and be able to defeat all disputants;and so on.

This completes the teachings on the six perfections found in *Clarifying the Sage's Intent* by Sakya Pandita. Simply by listening to these teachings, we have planted a seed in our mind-stream which has created a cause for us to deepen our understanding of the six perfections and accomplish them in the future. It has also become a cause for us to attain Buddhahood.

10

The Four Means of Gathering Followers

The fifth of the ten stages of practice expounded in the *Mahayanasutralamkara* is maturing sentient beings. The previous teaching explained the conduct of the six perfections, which is about perfecting one's own qualities. This section deals with bringing sentient beings to maturity through skilful means. There are four methods for maturing sentient beings:

(1) generosity;
(2) pleasant speech;
(3) beneficial conduct; and
(4) exemplary conduct.

(1) Generosity

This means giving followers the necessities of life in order to teach them religion. Avoiding incorrect generosity, we must please people through the correct practice of generosity, as explained earlier in the section on the perfection of generosity.

(2) Pleasant speech

This involves speaking pleasantly to beings and then leading them towards maturity by giving them appropriate teachings. Any words devoid of errors and harshness are considered to be pleasant speech. Even our greetings can be regarded as pleasing words to make others happy. Presenting the teachings correctly is also regarded as pleasant speech. The teachings we give should not conflict with scripture and reasoning. The definitive and provisional meanings should not be mixed up,[8] and we must not confuse the special, hidden and direct intentions of the teaching. Pleasant speech also covers teaching the Dharma with the proper motivation; in other words, not teaching with the motivation of gaining reward, fame or respect. We must teach purely for the sake of benefiting others.

(3) Beneficial conduct

Beneficial conduct involves working for the benefit of other beings, in order to lead them to engage in spiritual practices. The bodhisattva must help people to enter the practices fully, even if they initially lack the motivation and enthusiasm to undertake them as they were taught. We should encourage followers who fear they will be unable to practise, even after they have taken the vow of the enlightenment thought. For example, we might point out that it is said that some people who took the vow only because they were threatened by Vajrapani will nevertheless gain complete enlightenment. We should then explain, 'If they will gain complete enlightenment by taking the vow of the enlightenment thought only because they were threatened, what need is there to mention you, who take the enlightenment thought out of proper aspiration?' There is another story about how at one time Manjushri brought into his circle some disciples who did not have the correct motivation. When he asked them to take the enlightenment thought, some of them took it only to please him and some took it with the intention of deceiving him. Manjushri nevertheless bestowed the enlightenment thought upon all of them, and this eventually led them to practise properly.

Some may be reluctant to take the vow through fear of forgetting it later on. We should encourage such followers by explaining that even if they do forget the thought, the aspiration to attain awakening will not desert them. It is just like what happens when a person commits a great evil. Though he will forget this deed in later lives, he will still have to face the consequences in the future and will fall into the lower realms. In the same way, even if we forget the enlightenment thought after we have taken it, this does not mean we have abandoned it. We are just not being mindful of it for a

---

8   Teachings of provisional meaning require interpretation, whereas teachings of definitive meaning are intended to be taken literally.

certain period. Since we are planting the seed of the enlightenment thought, it will continue to grow in the future.

Some who have taken the bodhisattva vows think that they are unable to follow the path because they are incapable at this time of practising the six perfections. They need to understand that they are not expected to make these practices into the perfections right from the beginning. These perfections must be accomplished stage by stage. We can place these people on the path by explaining that generosity, morality and the other perfections must be practised in a gradual and steady way, not all at once.

(4) Exemplary conduct

The fourth method of bringing people onto the path is to act in accordance with the Dharma ourselves. For example, if you tell others that they must make offerings to Buddha or to the shrine, you yourself must be seen to make offerings. Or if you tell someone that he should listen to the Dharma when he does not wish to do so, you should also go and listen to the Dharma so that you can bring him along. By demonstrating to others that you are also practising what you teach, you will bring others with you onto the path. To illustrate this point, at one time a bodhisattva was walking along a road when he saw a woman carrying around the body of her dead child, because of her strong attachment to it. Wishing to help the woman, the bodhisattva went to a nearby cemetery, picked up a corpse at random and started carrying it around with him. When the woman saw him, she told him it was not seemly to carry a corpse around. The bodhisattva replied to her that she was right. He said he would abandon the corpse he was carrying if she would abandon the one she was carrying, too. Through the bodhisattva's act, the woman was brought to understand the futility of her behaviour and the pointlessness of her attachment to her dead child.

11

The Five Paths to Enlightenment

The text will now clarify the meaning of the sixth key phrase from the *Mahayanasutralamkara*, 'entering into the faultless levels' and 'purifying the fields.' This explains the five stages of the path and the ten bodhisattva stages. The phrase 'faultless levels' refers 'to the practices of the bodhisattva from the first up to the seventh stage of the bodhisattva path. 'Purifying the fields' refers to the eighth, ninth and tenth stages, during which the Mahayana practitioner engages in practices to purify his Buddha realm, such as Sukhavati. One might ask whether it is absolutely necessary to teach the five paths and the ten bodhisattva bhumis at this time, since we do not yet have the ability to understand them directly. The answer is that we must know about them as a prerequisite for developing spiritually and making progress on the paths to enlightenment. It's a bit like preparing to travel to another country; before we set off on our trip, we first prepare ourselves by trying to learn something about the place, the climate, the customs and so forth. The five paths are listed below.

(1) The path of accumulation

The first stage or gateway is the path of accumulation. On this stage one's mind becomes habituated for the first time to meditating generically on nonconceptual wisdom. We should be aware that the five paths are taught differently in the Hinayana and the Mahayana traditions. This text principally describes the paths according to the Mahayana tradition, which identifies three sections of the path of accumulation: the small, the intermediate and the great. When beings begin to meditate on the small path of accumulation, there is no certainty as to when they will develop the path of joining within their mind-stream. When their spiritual level progresses to the intermediate path of accumulation, it is certain that they will progress to the path of joining within a definite time frame. Once they develop the great path of accumulation, it means they will attain the path of joining within the current lifetime. If it is asked who are suitable candidates to attain the path of accumulation, the Hinayana teaches that this path can be attained only by a human being, either a male or a female of one of the three continents. No other living beings in this world system, such as gods, animals or humans lacking the proper organs, are able to gain the path of accumulation. According to the Mahayana, other sentient beings besides humans are also eligible to attain this path. If it is asked whether it is necessary to possess a meditative mind as a support to the path of accumulation, it is taught that this is not necessary. This is because even beings within the desire realm lacking this mind of meditative concentration have been able to accomplish this path. Therefore it is not necessary that the mind first be placed in one of the states of meditation in order to accomplish the path of accumulation.

It is said that whoever has taken the vows of the enlightenment thought out of great compassion and engages in the practices has entered the path of accumulation. There are many practices we must perform once we enter this path. There are numerous qualities which must be possessed by the person practising this path, and these may be subsumed into the following five principal categories:

(i)   maintaining proper morality;
(ii)   restraining the senses;
(iii) knowing how to limit one's intake of food;
(iv) being industrious in the sitting practices, by abstaining from sleeping at dawn and in the early part of the night; and
(v)   joyfully abiding in introspection—being aware of what should and should not be done.

(i) Maintaining proper morality

This means one must hold the vows one has taken as a monk, nun or lay person.

(ii) Restraining the senses

This means using wisdom to understand that whatever we perceive through our senses, such as forms through our eyes and sounds through our ears, is really empty by nature. With regard to method, it means that we always purify our actions and transform them into the quality of enlightenment. For example, as explained earlier: when we walk down the street, we can purify this activity by the thought, 'As I walk down this street, may all sentient beings enter the path to enlightenment,' and when we close the door, 'May all sentient beings close the door to the lower realms.' Thus we can purify the objects encountered by our senses.

(iii) Knowing how to limit one's intake of food

This means not taking food and drink with excessive desirous attachment and also limiting our intake. In other words, we must have the correct perception about why we are eating. We must bear in mind that we are eating to sustain the body in order to carry out the practices and to feed the various types of worms living inside it and so on. In such ways we can develop the appropriate attitude towards food and lessen our attachment to it.

(iv) Being industrious in the sitting practices, by abstaining from sleeping at dawn and in the early part of the night

Instead of sleeping excessively, we should devote part of our waking hours, such as the early evening and early morning, to meditation. We should meditate with a very stable mind on the impurities of the human body, the four strongly placed mindfulnesses (mindfulness of body, feelings, mind and dharma) or the various practices of the enlightenment thought.

(v) Joyfully abiding in introspection; being aware of what should and should not be done

A person on this path should possess not only mindfulness but also awareness or introspection. At the very time when he engages in any action, he should be aware whether the deed is concordant with his morality or not and whether it will accrue favourable or unfavourable results. He should apply this introspection during the performance of the deed and carry it out with this proper understanding. It is said that when one reaches the stage of the great path of accumulation, one attains certain miraculous or supernatural powers. One may even travel to the various Buddha realms to receive teachings directly from buddhas and bodhisattvas. The main practices on the path of accumulation are to listen to the doctrine, study it and contemplate the contents of the teachings, while upholding one's morality. The Sanskrit term for the path of accumulation is 'sambharamarga.' As to its etymological meaning, 'sambhara' means constantly practising or accumulating virtuous deeds again and again, while 'marga' means path.

(2) The path of joining or application

The path of joining or application is a higher gateway or path to liberation in which nonconceptualising wisdom is cultivated through generic characteristics (i.e. conceptual thought), based on what was previously achieved on the path of accumulation. At this stage one has not yet attained the actual realization of emptiness or selflessness, but there is a clearer mental vision of it, just as we can know about a certain place before we have been there. In other words, although one does not yet have the actual direct realization of emptiness or selflessness, one can meditate about it and work on the meaning.

There are three paths of joining: the small, the intermediate and the great. These divisions are similar to those of the path of accumulation. When there is no definite time as to when one will attain the path of seeing, which is the next path, this is known as the small path of joining. On the intermediate path of joining, there is a definite time frame for attaining the path of seeing. When one is on the great path of joining, one will attain the path of seeing within the current lifetime. The path of joining is also divided into four, according to the manner in which reality is realized. These four paths are:

(a) heat;
(b) peak;
(c) patient acceptance; and
(d) the most excellent mundane dharma.

(a) Heat

During the stage of heat, one continues to meditate with a clearer vision of emptiness. One still possesses only the generic realization of emptiness, which will not develop into actual nonconceptual realization until the path of seeing. Heat occurs as a sign heralding the arising of nonconceptual insight wisdom, just as the heat generated by rubbing two sticks together heralds the ignition of fire.

(b) Peak

When the meditation on emptiness develops further, though one still does not have direct realization, the clear vision of the generic realization of selflessness is progressively intensified. In other words, the mind is being steadied in this meditation. It is called 'peak,' because this is the last stage at which one's wholesome deeds remain shaky; from this time onwards, one's wholesome deeds become stabilized. The *Abhidharmakosha* explains this as the peak from which the root of one's virtuous deeds will never be cut by erroneous views—in other words, by disbelief in the law of karma and result.

(c) Patient acceptance

When one further intensifies the level of meditation on the generic meaning of emptiness and selflessness, one reaches the stage of patient acceptance. On this stage, the practitioner is no longer alarmed by emptiness and develops patience regarding the meditation itself.

(d) Most excellent mundane dharma

When one overcomes all forms of fear through this meditation on emptiness—in other words, when one overcomes the manifested conceptualisations which obstruct one from attaining the realization of emptiness—one reaches the fourth stage, known as the most excellent mundane dharma. However, one's realization of emptiness is still not completely accomplished. Although one has perfected all the different types of worldly dharmas, one has not yet attained the transcendental wisdom realizing emptiness. This is called 'the most excellent mundane dharma,' because it is the highest factor obtainable by worldly people. It acts as the predominant condition for attaining the undefiled path of seeing.

If it is asked who can attain the stages of the path of joining, according to Hinayana, anyone within cyclic existence born as a man or a woman with proper organs and anyone within the first six heavenly states of the desire realm can achieve this path. According to Mahayana, other beings are also suitable candidates to attain the path of joining. If it is asked what is the mental basis required to practise the path of joining, the answer is any of the six levels of form meditative concentration or meditative absorption. According to Hinayana, only the third of the four stages of the path of joining—that is, the path of patience—is divided into small, intermediate and great. However, according to Mahayana, each of these four paths is divided into small, intermediate and great. Therefore there are twelve levels on the Mahayana path of joining.

With regard to the realization of the path of joining, according to the two Hinayana schools, the paths of joining of shravaka and pratyekabuddha share the same object and cognitive mode. They realize the nature of the four noble truths, each of which has four aspects, such as impermanence, selflessness, etc. In other words, the sixteen aspects of the four noble truths are realized at this time. According to the Mind-Only school, during the first two parts of the path of joining, a clearer visionary realization of 'selflessness of things to be grasped,' or objective reality, is aroused during meditation. At the time of patient acceptance and the most excellent mundane dharma, there is clearer visionary realization of selflessness of the subjective aspect or grasper. Some great masters maintain that the path of joining of the bodhisattva is as follows: heat, the meditative absorption during which the illuminated insight is attained; peak, the meditative absorption in which the illuminated insight is intensified; patient acceptance, the meditative absorption in which one aspect of actual reality is entered into (selflessness-of-the-object aspect); and the most excellent mundane dharma, the meditative absorption in which the other aspect of actual reality is entered into (selflessness-of-the-subject aspect), immediately preceding the direct insight which will arise on the path of seeing.

The Sanskrit term for path of joining is 'prayogamarga.' 'Pra' is for 'paramārtha,' which means 'ultimate truth' or 'ultimate reality.' 'Yoga' means 'to join.' 'Marga' means 'path.' Therefore 'prayogamarga' means the 'path which joins to the path of seeing,' which directly sees the dharmadhatu, the ultimate reality. In other words, this second path, translated here as the path of joining or application, refers to the meditation uniting us with the realization of the state of ultimate reality, which will arise on the path of seeing.

(3) The path of seeing

The path of seeing is the union of meditative absorption and transcendental wisdom which sees the nature of the four noble truths directly. The path of seeing can also be classified into three types: the path of seeing of the Hinayana, the path of seeing of the Pratyekabuddhayana and the path of seeing of the Mahayana. In order to accomplish the path of seeing, we must relinquish the proximate (secondary) defilements and the root defilements. There are more or less twenty proximate defilements, such as stinginess, dishonesty, envy, etc. Since they are all based on the six root defilements, they will automatically be eliminated when the root defilements are overcome. The six root defilements are desirous attachment, anger, pride, ignorance, doubt and erroneous defiled view.

The general defining characteristic of defilement is 'that which disturbs the mind-stream,' preventing it from abiding in peace and calm. There are two broad categories of defilements: imputed defilements and innate defilements. Wrong views[9] which cannot be logically established are included in the category of imputed defilements. All ordinary beings, including shravaka and pratyeka aryas, possess innate defilements. These include desirous attachment to loved ones and hatred towards enemies and so on. According to the Hinayana teachings, all the imputed defilements are abandoned during the path of seeing, in one moment of meditation. The innate defilements are abandoned step by step during the path of meditation. According to Mahayana, bodhisattvas abandon all the obscurations of defilements on their path of seeing.

According to the *Abhidharmasamuccaya* (Compendium of Knowledge), the Abhidharma teachings of the Mahayana, there are ten defilements to be abandoned by the path of seeing. These are the

---

9   The five erroneous defiled views ('lta ba lnga') are: (1) the view of the transitory collection; (2) extreme views; (3) maintaining an inferior view as the excellent view; (4) holding the view of inferior moral conduct to be supreme; and (5) perverse views.

six root defilements: desirous attachment, anger, pride, ignorance, doubt and erroneous defiled view. The sixth of these is further subdivided into five, making ten. These are applied to the three realms of existence: the desire realm, the form realm and the formless realm. With regard to the desire realm, the ten are multiplied into forty through engaging in the four noble truths. Since the two upper realms, the form and the formless realm, lack anger, each has only nine. So when nine from each are multiplied through their engagement in the four noble truths, they total thirty-six each in the form and formless realms. All together, therefore, there are a hundred and twelve defilements to be abandoned by the path of seeing. The *Abhidharmakosha* of the Hinayana teaches that there are eighty-eight multiplied defilements to be abandoned on this path.

According to the Mahayana teachings, the Mahayana path of seeing is the meditational state of the first bhumi. The 'things to be abandoned' on this path are classified into two: the obscuration of defilements and the obscuration of phenomena. Both of these obscurations need to be totally eliminated in order for one to gain full and perfect enlightenment. It is said that the realization arising in meditation on the Mahayana path of seeing eliminates all the obscuration of defilements completely. With regard to the obscuration of phenomena, this can be divided into two categories: the obscurations to be abandoned on the path of seeing and the obscurations to be abandoned on the path of meditation. The first of these are uprooted along with the obscuration of defilements in meditation on the Mahayana path of seeing.

With regard to the physical basis or suitable candidate for the path of seeing, according to the Hinayana teachings, any male or female, as well as gods within the first six lower heavenly realms of the desire realm, are able to gain the path of seeing. According to the Mahayana, in addition to these beings, animals and others are also qualified to attain the path of seeing. From the perspective of the mental basis of the path of seeing, the Hinayana paths of seeing are based on any of the six form dhyanas, or meditative absorptions. The rhinoceros-like[10] pratyeka and Mahayana paths of seeing are based on the fourth or highest form dhyana.

---

10   So called because the pratyekabuddha is solitary, like the rhinoceros.

With regard to the manner of realizing the objects of the path of seeing, practitioners who possess the Hinayana path of seeing realize the selflessness of person through focusing on the four noble truths. Practitioners who possess the pratyeka path of seeing, in addition to realizing the selflessness of person, realize the selflessness of the outer objective aspect. Bodhisattvas on the path of seeing realize the selflessness of the person, the selflessness of the outer object phenomena and also the selflessness of the perceiver. In other words, their realization of selflessness or emptiness is complete.

The Sanskrit term for the path of seeing is 'darshanamarga.' 'Darshana' signifies that one sees or realizes the dharmadhatu, which was not previously seen. In other words, it means seeing the real nature of the four noble truths, or the emptiness of all phenomena, for the first time. According to the Mahayana, when one attains the Mahayana path of seeing, one attains the first bhumi; that is, the first arya bodhisattva stage. The Hinayana realist schools do not accept the ten bodhisattva levels. However, according to them, one becomes an arya or noble being on gaining the Mahayana path of seeing. Hinayana teachings classify noble Hinayana practitioners into distinct types of persons with distinct realizations, differently from Mahayana.

(4) The path of meditation

The path of meditation involves habituating the mind-stream in the path of special meditative absorption. In other words, one makes meditative absorption a habitual pattern so that it becomes part of one's being. There are two types of path of meditation: the mundane path of meditation and the supramundane path of meditation. The mundane path of meditation is shared by both Buddhists and non-Buddhists, but the supramundane path is exclusive to Buddhists. Ordinary humans and other beings have the path of meditation, but on the mundane level there is no such thing as the path of seeing. Since it is evident that we have all been born in the form and formless realms many times, the mundane path of meditation is common to all ordinary beings. This is because the causes for birth in the form and formless realms are mundane meditative absorptions. The mundane path of meditation is samatha. But samatha is essential also to the supramundane path, because it is the essential basis for developing all the higher paths to liberation.

Broadly speaking, the mundane path of meditation consists of samatha, not penetrative insight (vipashyana). Practitioners in all three yanas must develop samatha in order to attain their final goal. In the *Bodhicharyavatara,* the chapter on concentration is taught before the wisdom chapter, indicating that vipashyana is based on a strong foundation of samatha. Furthermore, Bodhisattva Shantideva says: 'Wisdom together with samatha enables a person to abandon all the defilements.' Therefore one should strive to acquire a strong practice of samatha. Samatha subsumes the four form states of meditation, or dhyanas,[11] and the four formless states of meditative absorption. For each of these states, there are seven preparatory steps. When the preparatory steps of each state have been completed, the respective actual meditative absorption is perfected. At least one if not all of these worldly actual meditations must be accomplished in order to make the mind firm and establish a proper state of one-pointedness. The teachings on the different states of form and formless meditation are very important, and many commentaries have been written about them.

Supramundane meditation involves habituating the mind in the realization of ultimate reality, to stabilize the realization gained during the path of seeing. Bodhisattvas who have gained the supramundane path of meditation may also engage in the mundane path of meditation in the post-meditative session, during which many thoughts arise in the mind, either related or unrelated to the supramundane meditation session. The supramundane path of meditation seeks to habituate the mind in the realization of emptiness, so that it adheres to the mind not only during meditation but also in the course of daily life.

With respect to the 'things to be abandoned' on the path of meditation, there are variations among the three yanas. According to the Hinayanist schools, there are fourteen defilements or 'things to be abandoned' on the path of meditation of all three yanas. According to the Madhyamika school, on the other hand, the

---

11 Of the four form dhyanas, the first dhyana has three parts and is counted as three, while the remaining dhyanas are counted as only one each.

Mahayana paths of meditation (second to tenth bhumis) discard only the obscuration of phenomena, since the bodhisattva has already uprooted the obscuration of all kinds of defilements while on the path of seeing, before developing his mind-stream into the path of meditation.

In terms of the suitable candidate for this path, the path of meditation will arise in males and females of three continents, excluding the northern continent. It will also arise in beings in the six classes of desire-realm gods, in form-realm beings (with the exception of the Great Brahma and certain beings on the fourth form realm known as long-life gods) and in beings in the formless realm (except for those on the highest peak). The reason why beings in the highest formless realm are not suitable candidates is that, in order to develop higher realization or achievement of meditative absorption, one needs to have a mind which looks down to the lower stage, seeing it as gross, and looks up to the stage above, seeing it as subtle and inspiring. But even though the peak of the formless realm looks down and considers the lower state to be gross, it does not have a stage above it to which it can look up for inspiration. Furthermore, the being on the peak of the highest formless realm has a dull mental state. The path of meditation cannot be attained by beings of the three lower realms, the northern continent, or neuters within the human realm.

With regard to the requisite mental basis, the paths of meditation of shravakas are based on any of the six form meditative absorptions and three kinds of formless meditative absorptions. The rhinoceros-like pratyeka path of meditation is based on the actual fourth form meditative absorption and the paths of meditation of the other type of pratyeka are based on any of the six form meditative absorptions. The bodhisattva paths of meditation are based on the extremely immaculate fourth form dhyana.

The Sanskrit term for the path of meditation is 'bhavanamarga.' 'Bhavana' means becoming familiarized with what one has previously realized or seen (that is, emptiness or selflessness).

(5) The path of no more learning

The fifth path is the path of complete accomplishment, known as the path of no more learning. It has three divisions: the path of no more learning of the Shravakayana, the path of no more learning of the Pratyekabuddhayana and the path of no more learning of the Mahayana. One who practises the shravaka path attains the Hinayana destination and becomes a shravaka arhat. One who practises the Pratyekabuddha path attains the pratyeka destination and becomes a pratyekabuddha. The path of no more learning of Mahayana, also known as complete and perfect Buddhahood, is the final destination for Mahayana practitioners. According to the Hinayana school, the physical and mental basis on which this path arises is the same as that of the supramundane path of meditation explained earlier. With regard to the common system shared by all the yanas, the shravakas' achievement of the final goal is as just explained, but the final achievement of the pratyekabuddhas and bodhisattvas will arise only on the basis of a human body.

In order for the bodhisattva to attain Buddhahood in his current lifetime, he must be born as a human being in the Brahmin or Ksatriya caste in the central country, Magadha, in the southern continent, Jambudvipa. The mental basis is the fourth meditative absorption of the form realm. This is the finest state of absorption, because one meditates on it again and again, and it becomes increasingly purer and finer. According to uncommon Mahayana, Buddhahood is attained on the physical basis of the tenth-bhumi bodhisattva. The mental basis is the vajra-like meditative absorption at the end of actualizing the extremely immaculate fourth form meditative absorption.

In brief, shravaka arhatship is achieved in all the realms—desire realm, form realm and formless realm—with the exception of certain states within the three realms. For instance, in the desire realm, shravaka arhatship is achieved either on the basis of the body of a human or that of a mundane god. Within the form realm, all god beings are eligible, with the exclusion of the Great Brahma and long-life gods. It can also be achieved in the formless realm. On attaining shravaka arhatship, one has already abandoned all the defilements of the three realms. If that state is attained on the basis of a form-realm or formless-realm body, there will be no suffering of suffering. However, if it is attained on the basis of a desire-realm body which has not yet gone to remainderless liberation, even though the shravaka arhat no longer has any defilements, he may still experience the suffering of suffering. However, he will have no further suffering after he passes away. There are some examples of shravaka arhats experiencing the suffering of suffering before attaining remainderless nirvana. For instance, one of the disciples always pictured at the side of the Buddha, Maudgalaputra, was beaten by non-Buddhist monks, even though he was renowned for his clairvoyance and miraculous displays. He suffered and died as a result. Also at the time of Buddha, there was another monk arhat named Char Ka, who, while giving a discourse on the faults of adultery, was beaten to death by a member of the audience who had a guilty conscience.

Shravaka arhats are not all the same. If a shravaka arhat is engaged in the actual meditative absorption of one of the form realms, then in addition to being free from defilements, he also possesses other qualities, such as clairvoyance, the ability to perform miraculous displays and so forth. But the qualities of shravakas are limited compared with those of buddhas. For example, arhats with such special powers are unable to see things which happened long ago in time or which are spatially far away. With regard to their clairvoyant ability to see into the future, this involves a considerable amount of effort on their part. They need to meditate again and again. In the case of the shravaka arhat Char Ka, although he possessed such qualities, he did not foresee that he would be killed by the adulterous person.

Pratyekabuddhas are higher than shravaka arhats. According to one of the Hinayana schools, the shortest possible time for achieving shravaka arhatship is three lifetimes, whereas the shortest possible time to attain the stage of pratyekabuddha is one hundred eons. There are two kinds of pratyekas: those who mingle with crowds and those who isolate themselves from others. The isolated, or rhinoceros-like, pratyekabuddhas isolate themselves not only physically but also vocally. When they go out to beg alms, they impart teachings to disciples and patrons by performing miracles. Pratyekabuddhas come into the world when all the sangha and shravaka disciples of the Buddha have left and the future Buddha has not yet appeared. In other words, pratyekabuddhas come into the world between appearances of fully enlightened Nirmanakaya buddhas.

Even when Hinayana schools describe the attainment of Buddhahood through the path of the bodhisattva, they mention only the selflessness of person. 'Selflessness of phenomena' is therefore a term used exclusively by the Mahayana schools. According to the Hinayana tenets, in addition to realizing the selflessness of person, the qualities of pratyekabuddhas, such as their clairvoyances, are much more powerful than those possessed by shravaka arhats. The Mind-Only school asserts that shravakas and pratyekabuddhas realize only the selflessness of person. According to one sub-school of the Madhyamika school, shravakas realize the complete selflessness of person, and in addition to that, pratyekabuddhas realize half the selflessness of phenomena. Another sub-school asserts that both shravakas and pratyekabuddhas realize the complete selflessness of both person and phenomena.

According to the Hinayana tenets, the historical Buddha Shakyamuni realized only the selflessness of person. He attained Buddhahood on the basis of a human body and was born in the royal caste. Hinayana does not accept any other Buddha besides Shakyamuni. With regard to Buddha's knowledge, they accept that he is omniscient, but they claim that he knows everything step by step. Hinayana schools say further that shravaka arhats, pratyekabuddhas and buddhas cease when they die, and there is no continuation. According to Mahayana, a Buddha has three bodies, or kayas: Dharmakaya, Sambhogakaya and Nirmanakaya. The Hinayana schools, on the other hand, do not accept three kayas. According to Mahayana—or, more specifically, the Madhyamika school—complete Buddhahood is attained within a very pure realm called Great Akanishtha, on the basis of the enjoyment body or Sambhogakaya. From that body, the Buddha emanates various forms, such as Shakyamuni Buddha. Manifestations of the Buddha are not exclusive; they will arise in every realm. In terms of abandonment, the complete and perfect Buddha has abandoned all possible obscurations, along with their residues.

With respect to the etymology of the phrase 'the path of no more learning,' the Sanskrit term for this path is 'asaiksa-marga,' which means 'completion.' This path brings to completion both the elimination of the things to be eliminated and the knowledge of phenomena. Therefore it is 'the path of completion.' Since it is free from defilements, it is also known as 'free from defilements.' Even though the path of no more learning does not abandon anything, since there is nothing left to abandon, it is also called 'the antidote,' because it prevents the defilements from returning.

12

The Ten Bhumis

The word 'stage' or 'bhumi' generally means level of spiritual attainment. Its defining characteristic is 'that which acts as the basis for excellent spiritual qualities.' There are two kinds: the bhumis engaged in through aspiration and the supramundane bhumis. According to the presentation on the bhumis by the Mahayana schools, there are differences between Hinayana and the Mahayana paths. Within the Hinayana path, there are eight stages to attain. These are the level of seeing the wholesome, the level of spiritual lineage, the level consisting of eight, the level of restraint, the level freed from desire, the level of mastery, the level of the shravaka and the level of the pratyekabuddha. Within the Mahayana, stages or bhumis are divided into two parts: the stages of ordinary practitioners and the stages of the noble aryas. The stages of the noble bodhisattva aryas are the ten stages of the bodhisattva path.

It is sometimes asked why there are neither more nor fewer than ten stages of the arya bodhisattva path. This is because, although the realization of ultimate reality arising from each of the ten stages is the same, the qualities which arise from the subsequent practices differ. Here, in order to gain the qualities of the subsequent practices on the bodhisattva path, the practitioner must accomplish the ten perfections. These ten perfections relate to the ten stages of the arya bodhisattva path. Each of these ten stages has the quality of being free from something. It may be said that they have crossed the four mighty rivers of suffering and are free from the five fears: lack of livelihood, untimely death, spreading of disrepute, evil destinies and lack of confidence in the midst of an assembly. One should understand by implication that these qualities increase gradually from the first level up to the tenth.

Even though arya bodhisattvas are free from fears and sufferings, they deliberately give the appearance of taking birth, growing old, becoming ill and dying in order to benefit sentient beings. They develop twelve sets of one hundred excellent qualities, which arise in a single moment on the first level. These are described in the *Dashabhumika Sutra* (Sutra on the Ten Grounds) in the following way:

(1) attaining one hundred meditative absorptions and dwelling in them;

(2) seeing one hundred buddhas;

(3) understanding the buddhas' sustaining powers;

(4) causing one hundred world realms to quake;

(5) going to one hundred pure realms;

(6) illuminating one hundred world realms;

(7) bringing one hundred sentient beings to spiritual maturity;

(8) dwelling for one hundred aeons;

(9) penetrating one hundred previous and subsequent aeons through supernormal intuition;

(10) opening one 'hundred doors of Dharma;'

(11) displaying one hundred bodies; and

(12) displaying one hundred bodhisattvas as the retinue of each of these bodies.

These excellent qualities are multiplied at each level. On the second level, this figure becomes one thousand; on the third level, it becomes one hundred thousand; on the fourth level, one hundred times ten million; on the fifth level, one thousand times ten million; on the sixth level, one hundred thousand times ten million; on the seventh level, ten million times ten billion. On the eighth level, their number is equal to the number of atoms in one hundred thousand world realms; on the ninth level, it is equal to the number of atoms of ten times one hundred thousand world realms; and on the tenth level, one attains excellent qualities equal to the number of atoms in inexpressibly many Buddha fields, in addition to other excellent qualities.

The word 'bhumi' literally means soil or ground. The significance of employing this word for the bodhisattva stages is that, just as the ground is the support for all things, animate and inanimate, the ten bhumis support all the myriad qualities attained by Mahayana practitioners who have reached the stages of the enlightening path. From the viewpoint of the Mahayana doctrine, the term 'bodhisattva bhumi' refers to the mental quality which is the unification of method and wisdom. In other words, when the wisdom realizing emptiness is merged with great compassion, this is known as the stages of the arya bodhisattvas.

(1) The first: Supremely Joyful

The first arya bodhisattva stage is called Supremely Joyful because the bodhisattva experiences the unification of method and wisdom for the first time. He sees the nature of reality directly and is very joyful about this. He joyfully engages in many supplications and prayers, especially the *Prayer of Samantabhadra*. He knows that he can now be of much more benefit to sentient beings, and he feels very happy about this. On this level the bodhisattva achieves the perfection of generosity.

(2) The second: Stainless

The bodhisattva becomes extremely pure and achieves the perfection of morality. He is now free from dualistic thought regarding 'true existence' of the three factors. Because of his thorough purity of body, speech and mind, he accomplishes the ten virtuous deeds in a complete way. It is said that from this stage onwards, he will be free from all immoral activity, even during dreams. There are some scholars who disagree that bodhisattvas dream at all after reaching the first bhumi, since dreams are a product of deluded mind. However, there are two responses to this. One is that although the bodhisattva may not actually have dreams, since he is able to appear in many different manifestations, including that of animals, why can't he appear as a human being who can dream? Another response is that it is just hypothetical, like the hypothetical postulation of a Buddha lacking compassion. In other words, supposing that the bodhisattva on the second bhumi were to dream, he wouldn't dream of immoral activity.

(3) The third: Luminous

It is said that the wisdom of the third bhumi is like a fire consuming the fuel of knowable objects, issuing forth rays of light in the process. For this reason the third bhumi is known as the Luminous or the Illuminator. It is likened to the sun. 'Knowable' means 'to be known.' As realization increases, there are fewer and fewer 'knowable objects' to be known. The bodhisattva has a vision of transcendental wisdom, which is similar to the colour of copper. So this stage is likened not only to the sun but also to the metal copper. The bodhisattva attains the perfection of patience.

(4) The fourth: Radiant

This bhumi is called the Radiant because the copper-coloured light first seen on the third bhumi becomes even more intense. The bodhisattva now engages primarily in the perfection of enthusiasm or joyous effort. All other qualities follow this, because without effort one cannot succeed in any kind of practice. It is the cause of both accumulations. In other words, effort is needed for accumulating both merit and wisdom. The bodhisattva now practices especially the thirty-seven practices of a bodhisattva, also known as the thirty-seven factors conducive to enlightenment. As a result of meditating on these, his meditational vision becomes even greater than that of a bodhisattva on the third bhumi.

(5) The fifth: Difficult to Conquer

This great bodhisattva cannot be defeated by maras. That is why this bhumi is known as Difficult to Conquer. The Tibetan name for the fifth bhumi is 'sbayang dka' ba,' which can also mean 'the one which is difficult to learn or to practise.' But here it means 'difficult to conquer.' On this bhumi, the bodhisattva's principal emphasis is on the perfection of meditative concentration. He gains deep realization of the four noble truths. Even though the bodhisattvas on the earlier bhumis also realize and understand the four noble truths, a bodhisattva on the fifth bhumi understands them in very precise detail. Because his meditation is so advanced, his realization of the four noble truths is also extremely advanced.

As the Mahayana practitioner progresses on the path, there are many negative forces trying to harm him. There is a saying that wherever there are people practising Dharma, there are forces trying to obstruct them. So one who engages in the practice of Dharma needs to have the skilful methods to oppose negative forces. Of course, the bodhisattva on the first bhumi has also gained the ability to tackle these negative forces. However, on the fifth bhumi, this ability becomes stabilized to the point at which negative forces are unable to prevail.

(6) The sixth: Directly Manifested

The Tibetan term for this stage is 'mngon du gyur pa', which may be translated into English as 'directly manifested.' It is also known as 'mngon du phyogs pa,' which means 'approaching.' From this stage onward, the perfection of wisdom is increasingly intensified. The bodhisattva abides in the practice of the perfection of wisdom, and he also sees the suchness or thatness of interdependent origination. By abiding in a more advanced perfection of wisdom, the bodhisattva is said to have attained cessation. This does not mean the state of liberation. It is not exactly like the state of cessation mentioned in the four noble truths. Here cessation means the negation of 'true' grasping,[12] which the bodhisattva has now attained, because the practice of the perfection of wisdom is so highly developed on this stage.

The opposite of wisdom is grasping, starting with 'true' grasping and succeeded by other kinds of grasping. 'True' grasping has already been cut off, but the residues of 'true' grasping and other kinds of conceptual grasping remain. The process of complete removal of conceptual grasping starts with the sixth bhumi, because of the bodhisattva's advanced practice of the perfection of wisdom. That is why he is said to have attained cessation. We can say that cessation and the perfection of wisdom go together, because the bodhisattva on this stage excels in the practice of wisdom.

(7) The seventh: Gone Far

This means gone far from conceptual grasping. The bodhisattva now achieves a special ability to get rid of conceptual discriminating grasping, such as thinking, 'this is male, this is female; this is white,

---

12   'True' grasping means conceiving all the objects of perception as truly existent.

this is blue,' and so forth. Because of the extent of this ability to abandon conceptual grasping, he is said to have 'gone far.' This ability begins to emerge in the bodhisattva on the sixth bhumi and culminates in the bodhisattva on the seventh bhumi. According to Gorampa,[13] this is the ability which most distinguishes this bhumi from the other six impure bhumis. Because of this attribute, when a bodhisattva attains the seventh bhumi, he will surpass the shravakas and pratyekabuddhas not only through merit but also through wisdom.

On this bhumi, the bodhisattva accomplishes the perfection of means. It is said that through his perfection of means, a bodhisattva on the seventh bhumi, as distinct from those on the previous stages, achieves the special ability to enter into and rise from meditative absorption, instant by instant.

(8) The eighth: Immoveable

Once the bodhisattva achieves the eighth bhumi, there is no reversing. He will go straight towards Buddhahood. This is because the enlightened mind does not need to conceptualise. It is placed on an unshakeable stage. Here one might well ask whether this means it is possible for bodhisattvas on the first seven bhumis to reverse; the answer is no. Not reversing is specifically mentioned here because from the eighth bhumi onwards, there is no conceptual grasping. On this stage there arise virtues superior to those of the preceding bhumis. Prior to the seventh bhumi, the bodhisattva attained virtues primarily through exerting effort. From the eighth bhumi onwards, although enthusiasm is present, effort is no longer required to carry out the practices.

The special perfection attained on this stage is the perfection of prayer or supplication. It was mentioned earlier that the bodhisattva on the first bhumi performs countless prayers, particularly the *Prayer of Samantabhadra*. This prayer is considered very important, since it includes all the other prayers. Now his prayers become even more effective, and all his prayers, including his earlier prayers, are answered. The bodhisattva remains in meditative equipoise in order to shed the abandonments of that stage with the aim of benefiting others. It is said that the Buddha 'wakens the bodhisattva from his

---

13 Go rams pa Bsod nams Seng ge (1429–1490)

meditation,' because once the bodhisattva has completely abandoned the things to be abandoned, there is no need to remain in that meditation any longer.

(9) The ninth: Good Intelligence

On the ninth bhumi, because of his superior perfection of force, the bodhisattva accomplishes the attribute of perfect understanding. It is said that there are four kinds of perfect understanding, known as the four individually correct cognitions (or correct cognizers). These are: perfect understanding of individual dharmas (terms), perfect understanding of individual meanings, perfect understanding of characteristics and perfect understanding of individual confidence. 'Perfect understanding of dharmas' means understanding all kinds of languages. 'Perfect understanding of individual meanings' refers to the complete meanings of all these words and expressions. 'Perfect understanding of characteristics' is the understanding of the individual characteristics of each phenomenon. 'Perfect understanding of confidence' is explained in various ways. Generally it refers to understanding the complex relationships between causes and results. The example usually given is the ability to understand the significance of the many colours on the feathers of a peacock. The bodhisattva on this stage understands why each colour is present and what has caused it. In the same way, however complex the results may be, he will understand the individual causes, without mixing one with another.

(10) The tenth: Cloud of Doctrine

The bodhisattva on the tenth stage accomplishes the perfection of transcendental wisdom. That is because all the obscurations have almost come to an end, and the more obscurations are abandoned, the brighter the transcendental wisdom becomes. This bhumi is called the Cloud of Doctrine, because it is like rain falling from the clouds and helping the crops to grow. The clouds are the bodhisattva's transcendental wisdom, the falling rain is the teaching of the Doctrine by the bodhisattva, and the growth of the crops is the increase in the virtues of living beings. Through his transcendental wisdom, the bodhisattva bestows teachings, and the living beings who receive his teachings develop virtuous seeds. That is why this bhumi is called the Cloud of Doctrine.

13

The Ultimate Result

The term 'Buddha' refers to one who has abandoned all the faults or impurities and has attained fully complete realization. The impurities referred to here are the two obscurations: the obscuration of defilements and the obscuration of phenomena. Buddha has completely discarded every defilement as well as all conceptual thoughts. By way of clarification, when the three lower aryas[14] overcome defilements, there is still a residue remaining. On the other hand, Buddha has overcome not only the roots of all impurities but also their residues. Therefore he is said to possess the perfection of complete relinquishment or abandonment of all impurities.

'Fully complete realization' refers to the fact that Buddha knows the true nature of all phenomena in addition to knowing all phenomena exactly as they are according to their conventional characteristics. One should be aware that realization has two aspects: one is to know what things are according to their ultimate nature and the other is to know all things as they are individually at the conventional level. Buddha possesses both of these omniscient cognitions. This is just a brief explanation of the meaning of complete perfection of realization.

The Kayas of Buddha

It is said that Buddha possesses three bodies, or kayas: Dharmakaya, Sambhogakaya and Nirmanakaya.

---

14   The 'three lower aryas' refers to shravaka aryas, pratyekabuddas and arya bodhisattvas.

(1) The Dharmakaya

The first kaya is known either as the Dharmakaya or as the Svabhavakaya. These terms refer to the non-differentiability of the two purities and the twenty-one classes of undefiled qualities acquired by Buddha. The two purities are primordial purity—that is, the natural purity of ultimate reality—and the purity consisting of being free from obscurations. The Svabhavakaya is also known as the Dharmatakaya. If we omit the syllable 'ta' from this word, between 'dharma' and 'kaya,' it becomes 'Dharmakaya.' So there should be no difference between 'Svabhavakaya' and 'Dharmakaya.' In brief, Dharmakaya refers to Buddha's transcendental wisdom, which possesses complete purity. This is because it is free from defilements, free from concepts and free from the residues of both.

(2) The Sambhogakaya (Enjoyment Body)

This is a Buddha residing in the pure Buddha realm, who is endowed with the five certainties, or definite features:

    (i)   'certainty of place' means Akanishtha;

    (ii) 'certainty of physical features' means adorned with the thirty-two major marks and eighty minor marks;

    (iii) 'certainty of teaching' means exclusively Mahayana teachings;

    (iv) 'certainty of retinue' means only bodhisattvas of the tenth bhumi; and

    (v) 'certainty of time' means unceasing, or for as long as samsara lasts.

(3) Nirmanakaya (Emanation Body)

The Nirmanakaya arises spontaneously from the Sambhogakaya. It dwells wherever there are disciples to be trained, whose number is said to equal the entirety of space. Its time frame is uninterrupted. All its activities are carried out for the sole purpose of benefiting beings. The Nirmanakaya may be further subdivided into three:

    (i)   birth Nirmanakayas, which appear in various kinds of births, such as the one dwelling in Tushita;

(ii) the highest emanations, or supreme Nirmanakayas, which are emanations in the form of Buddhas, such as Shakyamuni Buddha; and

(iii) artisan Nirmanakayas, the particular manifestations Buddha assumes in order to lead particular beings onto the path. An example is the violin player emanated by Shakyamuni Buddha in order to tame Supriya, the King of the gandharvas.

The Nirmanakaya and the Sambhogakaya may be collectively classed as Rupakaya, thus subsuming Buddha's kayas into two.

If it is asked whether or not Buddha has a mind, the answer is that Buddha does not have a mind, because he has completely eliminated adventitious stains. If it is asked whether Buddha has transcendental gnosis, the answer is that he has transcendental gnosis, because due to his omniscience, he is able to answer anything he is asked. This transcendental gnosis results from the complete transformation of his mental continuum at the time of full enlightenment.

Buddha's qualities

Ancient Indian scholars composed many verses about the Buddha's myriad qualities. His qualities are also described in two sections of special prayers or praises to Buddha, one by Maitreyanath and the other by Sakya Pandita. It is said that we can accumulate a lot of merit by reciting these texts daily.

The Special Qualities of Buddha Expounded by Maitreyanath
(1) The four immeasurables
The four immeasurables are loving-kindness or benevolence, compassion, joy in the happiness of others and equanimity. The first verse of praises composed by Maitreyanath refers to these four immeasurables. These may be broadly categorized into two: the intention to bring happiness to beings and the intention to benefit them. When we subdivide them two into four, the intention to bring happiness to beings is threefold: benevolence (the wish that beings meet with happiness); compassion (the wish that they be free from suffering); and sympathetic joy (the wish that they never be parted

from happiness and that they remain free from suffering). The last of the four is the intention to benefit beings by wishing that all beings live in equanimity—that is, in a balanced state of mind—without attachment to loved ones or hatred towards others.

(2) The eight liberations

Buddha's gnosis has the quality of eight liberations. These are various states of meditation. Ordinary people may attain some of these states of meditative absorption, such as the qualities of overcoming some of the defilements. Shravaka arhats and pratyekabuddhas can also attain various qualities of meditative absorption, by which they can overcome all the defilements. However, they do not overcome the obscuration of phenomena. The fully enlightened Buddha possesses all the qualities of meditative absorption, because he has achieved a state of meditation which completely eliminates both the obscuration of defilements and the obscuration of phenomena.

(3) Dignified suppressions

The sun suppresses the stars in a dignified and majestic way, so that when the sun shines, although the stars remain in the sky, we cannot see them. In a similar way, through various states of meditative absorption, Buddha performs miracles to help all sentient beings. Though others may be able to perform some of these, they cannot accomplish them in such a magnificent or wonderful manner as Buddha can. When Buddha performs miracles, the miracles of others pale into insignificance, just as the moon and the stars fade from the sky on a sunlit day.

(4) The ten pervasive concentrations

This refers to the qualities of Buddha's meditative absorptions and their activities. Through various meditative states, he can perform innumerable kinds of miracles. Further, through his transcendental wisdom or omniscience, he knows everything there is to know in the world. Though others can perform certain miracles or know some of the things in the world, no one else knows everything. Buddha knows each and every phenomenon in its entirety. Buddha's realizations are inexhaustible and free from all opposing factors.

(5) Non-afflictive concentration

Through his meditation, a shravaka arhat can stop a particular person from manifesting a particular defilement towards him. For example, if a person is angry with him, the arhat can curtail that anger. However, he is able to counteract only the one defilement directed towards him. On the other hand, through his meditation, Buddha can pacify all the manifested defilements of anyone who arouses desire or hatred, etc., towards him.

(6) Knowing from prayers

When a shravaka arhat is asked about the future, he does not need to throw dice to make a prediction. He need only make the effort of entering into a state of meditative absorption. However, if Buddha is asked the same question, he does not even need to enter meditative absorption or make any effort at all. He can answer without hesitation. Moreover, whereas the shravaka arhat knows only a part of the future, Buddha knows everything. Thus he can dispel all doubts.

(7) Four individually correct cognitions

(i) *Perfectly cognizing individual phenomena*
Buddha knows all phenomena according to their individual conventional characteristics. For example, Buddha knows the defining characteristics of all kinds of forms and all the varieties of mental states.

(ii) *Perfectly cognizing individual classifications*
Buddha knows in exact detail all the varieties of phenomena.

(iii) *Perfectly cognizing individual etymologies*
He knows how to explain all phenomena without intermingling them.

(iv) *Perfect confidence to explain all these*
He does not lack confidence to explain to people what the different things in the world are.

(8) Six clairvoyances

(i)   Buddha can perform miracles through his meditative state.

(ii) He knows the minds of others and whether or not they possess defilements.

(iii) He has clairaudience. With his supernatural power of hearing, he can hear any sound from anywhere, even from the ends of the universe.

(iv) He knows his past lives as well as the past lives of all sentient beings.

(v)   He can see the time, manner and place of death and rebirth of every living being and the nature of their future births.

(vi) He has the supernatural power of knowing the 'exhaustion of defiled states.' In order to help beings, Buddha knows the specific means by which each being can overcome his defilements and gain the state of liberation.

(9) The major and minor bodily marks

Because his body possesses the thirty-two major and eighty minor marks, he inspires confidence in all who see him. An example of the major marks is the protuberance on top of Buddha's head. An example of the minor marks is his slightly copper-coloured fingernails.

(10) The four thorough purities

(i)   *Thorough purity of the basis*
      Buddha can take birth whenever he wishes, in any body he chooses, and remain as long as he wishes.

(ii) *Thorough purity of object*
      Buddha has complete mastery over the various objective realities. For example, he can make existing things disappear and nonexisting things appear. In fact, he can do whatever he wants with things in order to help sentient beings.

(iii) *Thorough purity of enlightened thought*
Since he is free from all evils and has accomplished all merits, Buddha can enter into all the meditative absorptions and use them at will.

(iv) *Thorough purity of transcendental wisdom*
Because he has severed the continuum of ignorance, Buddha has mastered transcendental wisdom, completely free from obscurations, with regard to all phenomena.

(11) The ten powers

These ten powers apply specifically to various kinds of realization or knowledge.

(i) *The power of understanding proper and improper cause*
Some scholars have translated this into 'possible and impossible,' but 'proper and improper cause' is a better translation. By way of illustration, when a person experiences happiness, Buddha knows which particular virtuous deed resulted in that happiness and that nonvirtuous deeds are not the source of happiness.

(ii) *The power of understanding karmas and their consequences*
This is knowledge of the results corresponding to the range of virtuous and non-virtuous deeds. Buddha can see the specific relationship of causes and results in each instance.

(iii) *The power of understanding the various aspirations*
Buddha knows the multiplicity of aspirations possessed by disciples, such as worldly happiness and liberation.

(iv) *The power of understanding the various natural temperaments*
Buddha knows the desires and thoughts of individual sentient beings. He knows who belongs to the category of small, who belongs to the category of medium and who belongs to the category of great. In other words, he knows the temporary race of each person, whether it be shravaka, pratyeka or bodhisattva.

(v) *The power of understanding the various classes of mental faculties*
Buddha knows exactly who has the faculty of faith or enthusiasm and also whether their level of faith or enthusiasm is great, medium or inferior.

(vi) *The power of understanding the various paths leading to their corresponding destinations*
Buddha knows all the different paths and their corresponding results: the various worldly states and liberations.

(vii) *The power of knowing all the defiled and immaculate meditative concentrations*
Buddha knows all the kinds of meditative absorptions for gaining insight into all levels of worldly existence and also into the spheres of the levels of enlightenment.

(viii) *The power of knowing prior births*
Buddha knows not only his own previous births, but also the previous births of all sentient beings, including when, how and where they were born in their previous lives.

(ix) *The power of knowing dying and rebirth*
Buddha knows the death and rebirth of every sentient being, including when, how and where they will die and when, how and where they will be reborn.

(x) *The power of knowing the exhaustion of defilements*
Buddha knows the extinction of all the obscurations and their latencies. Consequently he reveals the methods for overcoming them to others who wish to learn about it.

(12) The four kinds of fearlessness

These are also known as Buddha's four grounds of self-confidence. They are: (i) fearlessness to assert that he has extinguished all negativities; (ii) fearlessness to assert that he has attained complete and perfect realization; (iii) self-confidence to reveal the paths of the antidotes for the purpose of others; and (iv) self-confidence to reveal the things to be discarded for the purpose of others. The first two of these pertain to his own purpose and the latter two pertain to benefiting others.

With regard to the first of these four, the Buddha is devoid of fear that anyone will challenge him or debate with him, and consequently he can proclaim in the midst of the proud that he is a completely enlightened being. With regard to the second, he has the ability to proclaim in the same manner that he has overcome all the obscurations. By contrast, if we claimed to be omniscient beings, we would be afraid that others might challenge us and prove us wrong.

The third and fourth kinds of fearlessness relate to others. With regard to the third, Buddha has no fear about informing beings that the path leading to worldly existence and suffering consists of deeds based on ignorance and rooted in self-grasping. With regard to the fourth, he can proclaim the path leading to liberation. He can state, for example, that through realizing the selflessness of person and the selflessness of phenomena, we can gain realization leading to complete liberation and omniscience. He is not afraid that anyone will challenge him, because he has complete understanding of the path and how to help others attain the state of liberation.

(13) The quality of not possessing three concealments
Since Buddha's body, voice and enlightened thought are completely purified and enlightened, he does not conceal any of his activities from others.

(14) The quality of applying three kinds of mindfulness
Buddha does not develop special liking for people who listen to his teachings attentively or anger towards those who don't—for example, people who fall asleep. He neither likes nor dislikes anyone, as his mind is always in equanimity. He consequently attracts disciples in an excellent way.

(15) Completely eliminating all the residues
Though certain lower enlightened beings, such as shravaka arhats, have overcome the defilements, they have not eliminated their residues. This may be likened to washing away the dirt on a shirt but not removing the stains. In consequence, shravaka arhats continue to engage in faulty physical and verbal action. For example, while walking along a road, they may by chance tread on a snake and be bitten, accidentally bump into an elephant, be hit by a car or fall over a cliff. On the other hand, the fully enlightened buddhas possess

complete omniscience at all times, regardless of what they do. Therefore there can never be any fault in the activities they perform from any of the three doors of actions.

(16) Quality of non-forgetfulness

From time to time we ordinary people forget the time we are supposed to meet someone, or what we have planned to do next. Even arhats sometimes forget things, since they do not have complete remembrance of everything they are supposed to do. However, the fully enlightened Buddha knows, for example, exactly when he is supposed to meet someone, what he is supposed to do and where he is supposed to be. There is no question that he will ever forget anything.

(17) Great compassion

It is said that Buddha looks with compassion upon all sentient beings of all the worldly realms three times during the day and three times at night. This is merely a figure of speech, because Buddha actually looks with compassion upon all sentient beings at all times, day and night, in order to lead them through the various paths to liberation. When the conditions are ripe for him to manifest and lead beings out of the hell realms or from worldly existence, he does so.

(18) The eighteen qualities exclusively possessed by complete buddhas

According to the Hinayana tradition, this refers to the eighteen special qualities of Buddha we have already mentioned; namely, the ten powers, the four kinds of fearlessness, the quality of applying three kinds of mindfulness and great compassion. However, according to Mahayana, this is a separate set of eighteen qualities exclusive to Buddha. These comprise six qualities of conduct, six qualities of realization, three qualities of transcendental wisdom and three qualities of transcendental activities.

(a) The six exclusive qualities of Buddha's conduct

(i) Free from physical errors

This is similar to what was mentioned above. For example, Buddha never makes bodily mistakes such as stepping on a snake or falling over a cliff.

(ii) Free from nonsensical utterances
Whereas a shravaka arhat, for example, may shout or laugh in an improper way, Buddha never makes such mistakes with his voice, as he has complete control over it and knows how to use it properly.

(iii) Never possesses non-meditative states
When a shravaka arhat awakens from meditation, he perceives the world differently from the way he perceives it during the meditative session. Thus shravaka arhats experience two states of being: one during sitting meditation and the other when they are out of meditation; in other words, during the post-meditative session. By contrast, Buddha's thoughts are permanently in a state of dharmata; he does not alternate between meditation and post-meditation.

(iv) Never has lapses of memory
Whereas a shravaka arhat may forget certain things, Buddha does not forget anything under any circumstances.

(v) Never possesses differentiating perception
Shravaka arhats perceive cyclic existence as a state of suffering to be abandoned and nirvana as a state of complete bliss to be attained. Buddha does not see in dualistic terms such as good and bad. This non-differentiating mode of realization is absent among lower enlightened beings, such as shravaka arhats.

(vi) Never being neutral without having examined the being
individually
Shravaka arhats observe sentient beings from time to time to decide whether they can help them or not, but they do not do so constantly. If they don't think they can help particular beings, they leave them alone. On the other hand, Buddha observes all sentient beings at all times, regardless of the circumstances, to see whether or not he can help them. If upon investigation he finds he cannot help a particular being at that time, he does not do anything, because the conditions are not ripe. When he sees that the person can be helped, he uses whatever means are appropriate. The distinction here is that Buddha observes all sentient beings at all times with a view to helping them, whereas other enlightened beings such as shravaka arhats, not to mention ordinary humans, do not do so all the time.

(b) The six unshared qualities of realization

With regard to transcendental wisdom, complete buddhas possess six qualities which can never be impaired. These are: aspiration, enthusiasm, mindfulness, wisdom, meditative absorption and the absence of all faults.

(c) The three transcendental wisdoms

This refers to Buddha's perfect knowledge of all past, present and future events through his omniscience.

(d) The three transcendental activities of body, voice and transcendent mind

It said that although shravaka arhats engage only in virtue, some of their actions may become neutral deeds owing to mental speculation. This wastes their time and effort. On the other hand, all deeds performed by Buddha are always based on transcendental wisdom and practised simultaneously with transcendental wisdom. In other words, none of Buddha's deeds are ever wasted.

(19) Being omniscient in every respect

The Dharmakaya is by nature pure and free from what is to be eliminated; that is, the adventitious stains of the two obscurations. The Sambhogakaya teaches the Mahayana to bodhisattvas on the tenth stage in Akanishtha, and the Nirmanakaya continually achieves the benefit of sentient beings through 'birth emanations,' 'highest emanations' and 'artisan emanations.' By the profundity of the Dharmakaya and the vastness of the two form kayas, Buddha understands phenomena exactly as they are and in all their varieties. Thus he can resolve the doubts of all sentient beings.

(20) Full accomplishment of the six perfections

Buddha has fully accomplished the six perfections and has overcome all the forces which obstruct them. For example, with regard to generosity, Buddha has accomplished the entire perfection of generosity and has defeated all obstructing forces, such as attachment to the object he is giving. With regard to his accomplishment of the perfection of morality, there is not the slightest defect. Similarly, Buddha has accomplished the remaining four perfections. Although it is said that bodhisattvas have accomplished the six perfections, they have not overcome the residual faults.

These are the twenty exclusive qualities of Buddha expounded in the *Mahayanasutralamkara* by Bodhisattva Maitreyanath. In *Clarifying the Sage's Intent*, Sakya Pandita lists fourteen additional qualities.

Fourteen Additional Qualities of Buddha Listed by Sakya Pandita
(1) Marvellous accomplishment of two purposes
Because Buddha has attained all the common and uncommon attainable qualities, he has accomplished the purposes of self and others without remainder and realizes all phenomena without exception.

(2) Thorough accomplishment of the thirty-seven factors of enlightenment

- Thorough accomplishment of the four strongly-placed mindfulnesses. This means examining the states of the body, feelings, mind and phenomena, to understand that they are empty by nature.
- The four correct endeavours.
- Accomplishment of four legs or causes of miracles. This refers to the attainment of certain miraculous powers or abilities arising from the four meditative states known as the four legs of miracles: aspiration, effort, thought and analysis.
- Accomplishment of the five spiritual faculties: the faculty of faith, the faculty of enthusiasm or effort, the faculty of mindfulness, the faculty of concentration and the faculty of wisdom.
- Accomplishment of the five powers. The powers arise when the opposites of the five spiritual faculties are completely eliminated. For example, when one does not fall under the opposite, such as not having faith (in opposition to having faith) and laziness (in opposition to enthusiasm).
- Accomplishment of the seven branches of enlightenment, which include wisdom and the other aspects.
- Accomplishment of the eight branches of aryas' path (or eightfold noble path), such as right view.

With regard to these, shravaka arhats and pratyekabuddhas possess the minimal accomplishment. Only perfectly enlightened buddhas possess the excellent accomplishment of the thirty-seven factors.

(3) The nine stages of meditation

The nine meditative absorptions are the eliminations of the nine conceptual thoughts of the three realms, from the relatively coarse to the relatively subtle. Eliminating the conceptual thinking of the desire realm is the first meditative concentration, and likewise it is the meditative attainment of the second, third and fourth concentrations of the form realm. The elimination of conceptual thinking of the form realm consists of four stages: infinite space, infinite cognition, nothing at all and neither existence nor nonexistence, which are formless meditative absorptions. The meditative absorption of cessation is the ninth meditative absorption, which blocks off all conceptual thought. Shravakas engage in the ninth meditative absorption in order to render their minds supple and serviceable and to extinguish their anguish over the various appearances and so forth of ordinary existence; bodhisattvas practise it to gain mastery over meditative absorptions; and Buddha achieves it spontaneously, through his total mastery of meditative absorption.

Although lower arhats also possess these nine states of meditation, shravaka arhats have to employ great effort to enter into them and arya bodhisattvas also need to exert effort, although less than that required by shravaka arhats. On the other hand, Buddha does not need to make any effort at all. He can enter into the nine meditative absorptions spontaneously.

(4) The three doors to liberation

This refers to the doors of emptiness, wishlessness and signlessness:

- Because he possesses wisdom which does not conceive either apprehended object or apprehending subject—in other words, does not conceive duality—Buddha has attained the door of emptiness.
- Because he possesses wisdom free from attachment to the five perpetuating aggregates, Buddha has attained wishlessness.

- Because he possesses wisdom which has gone beyond the conceptual mode, Buddha has attained marklessness or signlessness.

It is taught that the lower arhats and the arya bodhisattvas have also attained these three doors of liberation, but they have not, however, eliminated the obscurations of latent propensities. Since the complete Buddha has eliminated these, his three doors are supreme.

(5) Eradication of the four maras

- The first mara is the mara or demon of defilements such as desire, anger, ignorance, jealousy and miserliness.
- The second mara is the mara of aggregates, meaning the defiled aggregates, such as our mind and body, which arise due to the defilements and due to conceiving things as inherently existent.
- The third mara, the mara of death, refers to the moment of dying through the force of defiled karma and defilements.
- The fourth mara is known as the mara of the son of the god, which refers to heavenly beings who obstruct those who are engaged in the Dharma path for the purpose of defeating the first three maras.

All the afflictions are eradicated through attaining the realization of ultimate reality and the state of transcendental wisdom. When the afflictions of desire, anger and ignorance are eliminated, the first mara, the mara of defilements, is vanquished. When all the defilements have been eradicated, it is not possible to take birth through their power. When one no longer takes birth through their power, the mara of aggregates is vanquished. As a consequence, when one no longer takes birth, it is not possible to die. Thus the mara of death is vanquished. So the first three—the maras of defilements, aggregates and death—are eradicated along with their latencies by the Buddha's transcendental wisdom. The fourth mara, the mara of the son of the god, is eradicated along with its latencies by Buddha's accomplishment of great compassion. Great compassion arises from loving-kindness. Since Buddha sees every living being as his only child through the eyes of great compassion, no one opposes him. Therefore he does not perceive any external force such as the son of the god as an enemy or creator of obstacles. Because he has transformed his perspective, he does not see other beings as creating obstacles but rather as objects for his loving-kindness and compassion, just as if they were his only son. Thus he has also vanquished the mara of the son of the god. In this way, Buddha has overcome all four maras.

According to the Hinayana school, when Buddha Shakyamuni attained enlightenment under the bodhi tree at Bodhgaya, he eradicated the mara of defilements and the mara of the son of the god. Later on at Shravasti, at the time when Buddha was about to die but decided to extend his life for another three months in order to help others, it is said that he overcame the mara of death. Then at the time of his passing away at Kushinagar, since he would never take another defiled physical body of aggregates, it is said that he destroyed the mara of aggregates. According to the Hinayana school, he destroyed all the maras in this way.

According to the Mahayana, when Buddha Shakyamuni appeared in the world, there were no maras for him to destroy; he had already eliminated them at the end of the tenth bhumi.

(6) The ten dominions

(i) The first is dominion over life span. Buddha can remain in the world for as long as he chooses. He cannot pass away accidentally at any other time. This is the outcome of having prolonged the lives of sentient beings through his generous gifts of wealth.

(ii) The second is dominion over the mind. This is the serviceability of the Buddha's mind to enter into any absorption exactly as he wishes. It is the outcome of having satisfied the minds of others through generosity.

(iii) The third is dominion over material goods. Buddha can acquire material goods exactly according to his wishes. This is the outcome of having satisfied others with material goods.

These first three powers are the outcome of Buddha's generosity.

(iv) The fourth is dominion over activities or deeds. This is Buddha's ability to achieve deeds of body, speech and mind just as he wishes. It is the consequence of having impelled others to faultless deeds of body, speech and mind by means of his own moral discipline.

(v) The fifth is dominion over birth. Buddha is able to take birth anywhere within worldly existence, as a human being, god or whatever form he wishes to take. He has complete control over his birth in this world and also over how he will appear; for example, whether he appears in a beautiful form or in an ugly form. His realization of the aspirations endowed with moral discipline is the causal condition for this power.

(vi) The sixth is dominion over aspiration. This means that Buddha can create whatever he wants. For example, he can turn a piece of earth into gold. It is the result of acting in accord with the likings of sentient beings by means of patience.

(vii) The seventh is dominion over prayer or dedication. Whatever prayers Buddha makes for the benefit of beings will be accomplished. This is the result of having accomplished benefits for sentient beings in exact agreement with their wishes, through his enthusiasm.

(viii) The eighth is dominion over miraculous manifestations. Buddha can manifest in various forms in order to help sentient beings who are in need of these particular forms. This is the result of having undertaken higher paths exactly in accordance with the Doctrine, through meditative absorption.

(ix) The ninth is dominion over transcendental wisdom. Buddha has accomplished the entire realization of ultimate reality. This is the result of having applied himself to accomplishing whatever beings desire, through discriminating understanding.

(x) The tenth is dominion over Dharma. Buddha is able to teach whatever is in the three baskets of teaching— morality, sutra and wisdom, according to the needs of the listener. This is the result of having given religious instructions through the perfection of discriminating understanding.

(7) The quality of various states of meditative absorption

These meditative absorptions are superior to others; they don't depend on others and they are unimpeded. They may be broadly categorized into two kinds: those which deal with eliminating all the faults and those which deal with accomplishing all the qualities or realizations. There are many kinds of meditative absorptions within these two categories; for example, the jewel mudra, which refers to the accomplishment of various qualities to benefit others, and the vajra-like meditative absorption, which refers to a state of meditation by which all the defilements are completely pacified. Buddha has accomplished innumerable kinds of meditative absorptions.

(8) The door of dharani or non-forgetfulness

This refers to the quality of non-forgetfulness. For example, Buddha never forgets anything that has been said to him. It also refers to the quality of retaining all aspects of the Dharma so that he can teach any aspect of the Doctrine.

(9) The quality of consummate abandonment

Buddha has abandoned the obscuration of defilements, which blocks the attainment of liberation, and the obscuration of phenomena, which blocks the mind from transforming into omniscience. There are two aspects to each of these obscurations: one is the actual obscuration itself and the other is the residue remaining after the obscuration has been eliminated. For example, if you place a piece of cloth which has been scented with perfume on a table, some scent will remain behind after the cloth is removed. In the same way, even when we have eliminated all the defilements from the root, there is still a slight residue remaining behind. However, the Fully Enlightened One has completely eliminated both the obscuration of defilements and the obscuration of phenomena, together with their residues.

(10) The perfection of transcendental wisdom

Transcendental wisdom means the complete perfection of wisdom. Buddha has complete realization. According to the teachings of the Paramitayana, Buddha possesses four types of transcendental wisdom:

(i) Mirror-like wisdom

Buddha knows all the things to be known in this world system clearly, like objects reflected in a mirror. With regard to the other three wisdoms, mirror-like wisdom is the support and the ensuing three wisdoms are the supported.

(ii) The wisdom of equality

Buddha has completely transcended the dualistic grasping of subject and object. He abides in this non-dual state, which means that his wisdom always remains in equilibrium.

(iii) Discriminating wisdom

This is the treasure of all excellent qualities, such as the powers and the ways of fearlessness.

(iv) The wisdom of accomplishing beneficial deeds

This means spontaneously realizing all the beneficial activities for self and others.

Buddha's infinite qualities of wisdom may be subsumed into two: the omniscience of the ultimate state of being and the omniscience which consists of knowing all phenomena individually. Even such qualities as the Buddha's ten powers and four kinds of fearlessness come under the category of transcendental wisdom. Although they are one in nature, they may be classified into these two aspects, due to their different focusing objects.

(11) The excellent qualities of speech

Buddha possesses sixty excellent qualities of speech. His speech is gentle, pleasing, without fault and can be heard from a great distance. By means of these qualities of speech, when he teaches, he is able to lead gods, men and all eligible beings onto the path of liberation.

(12) The quality of transformation

This refers to complete transformation of the impure states of the five aggregates, the twelve elements and the eighteen spheres into the pure transcendent state.

(13) The quality of wealth

Buddha has a wealth of enlightened qualities such as wisdom, miraculous powers and miraculous emanations. It is said that if we were to take all the worldly wealth possessed by great heavenly beings such as Shakra and Brahma, however great they might seem to us, they would be outshone by the spiritual wealth possessed by a single arhat. The spiritual wealth possessed by all the arhats is outshone by the greater spiritual wealth of a single pratyekabuddha. The spiritual wealth possessed by all the pratyekabuddhas is outshone by the greater spiritual wealth of a single bodhisattva. The spiritual wealth of all bodhisattvas is far outshone by the greatest spiritual wealth, that of the fully enlightened Buddha.

To illustrate the point regarding the quality of wealth, at one time there was an arhat by the name of Arya Upagupta. A demon or Mara was trying to obstruct him. The demon approached Upagupta and mocked him by offering him a garland of flowers. But the arya took the rosary and placed it around the demon's neck. The rosary then transformed itself into the corpse of a dog infested with maggots. No matter how hard the demon struggled to remove it, he could not, so he became very distressed. He promised the arya that he would never again cause problems to those on the path of Dharma and that he would henceforth protect them. After that he was able to remove the dog's corpse.

There is a story to illustrate the difference between the shravaka arhat's qualities and those of the bodhisattvas. At one time, when many world systems were being destroyed by fire, Manjushri and Shariputra went from one world system to another, right up to the end of the three worlds of existence. Manjushri suggested to Shariputra that they return by miraculous means in order to arrive quickly. So he asked Shariputra, 'Will we return using your miraculous powers, or do you want me to use mine?' Shariputra was curious to see what a Mahayana practitioner could do, so he suggested Manjushri use his powers. Manjushri said to Shariputra, 'In that case, close your eyes.' But even before Shariputra managed to close his eyes completely, Manjushri said, 'Now open them.' They were right back where they had started! Shariputra observed to Manjushri that his power must be very great to accomplish such a feat in so short a time. Manjushri replied, 'My conduct is not within the domain of shravakas such as you, who posses inferior aspiration.'

(14) Buddha is the excellent refuge

From among the qualities of the Buddha explained above, the immeasurables, emancipations, bases of dominion, bases of exhaustions and five of the clairvoyances are qualities shared by some worldly beings. Buddha's sixth clairvoyance, his absence of defilements, his knowledge resulting from resolution, four individually correct cognitions, thirty-seven factors conducive to enlightenment, nine meditative attainments, three doors to liberation, etc. are shared with shravaka arhats. Other qualities such as miraculous powers, meditative absorptions and some transformations, etc. are shared with bodhisattvas on the seven impure bhumis. Qualities such as transformation of defiled consciousness and the major and minor physical marks are shared with bodhisattvas on the eighth bhumi. The door of dharani or unforgetfulness and the great four individually correct cognitions are shared with bodhisattvas on the ninth level. Some qualities such as ten dominions, etc. are held in common with bodhisattvas on the tenth level.

In addition to all these, there are certain qualities unique to Buddha. These include the eighteen special qualities possessed by no one else: that is, the six qualities of behaviour, the six qualities of realization, the three qualities of transcendental wisdom and the three qualities of transcendental activities described earlier. Since Buddha has attained all the common and uncommon qualities, he is the most supreme refuge.

The scriptures explain the qualities of Buddha in many ways. According to the *Prajnaparamita*, the Dharmakaya of Buddha has twenty-one sets of qualities and his Rupakaya has thirty-two major and eighty minor marks. According to the *Mahayanasutralamkara* by Maitreyanath, Buddha has twenty sets of special qualities. According to Sakya Pandita, in addition to these, there are an additional fourteen.

Some of Buddha's qualities are described to enable us to accumulate merit and also to induce us to produce faith in Buddha. In actuality, we would never be able to describe every quality Buddha possesses, because his qualities are inconceivable and infinite. It would be impossible on the basis of the merits we possess to understand Buddha's qualities. Therefore these lists are merely partial descriptions.

As you have now received the entire teaching, this has placed the seed of the complete path to Buddhahood in your minds. It is said that a great amount of merit is accumulated whenever we listen to the Doctrine. When we are on our way to hear a Dharma teaching, every time we put our foot down we take a step nearer to the place where the Dharma is being taught. Therefore we accumulate merit with every step. If we drive a car to the teachings, we accumulate merit every time we hit the accelerator. Since we have been able to accumulate such great merit by listening to this teaching, or by reading and contemplating upon it, we should dedicate all the merit and transform it into the basis to gain enlightenment for the sake of all sentient beings.

Glossary

Abhidharma (*chos mngon pa*)
The wisdom teachings of Buddha. The third of the Tripitaka (three baskets) of Buddha's teachings.

aggregates, five (*phung po lnga*)
These are the five 'heaps' or 'skandhas' of psychophysical phenomena: forms, feelings, discriminating perception, compositional factors and consciousness.

arhat (*dgra bcom pa*)
Literally, 'foe destroyer.' This term refers to all three enlightened beings: Hinayana followers who have reached the path of no more learning of Hinayana, pratyekabuddhas and complete buddhas.

Asanga (*thogs med*)
Asanga was a Mahayana master believed to have been born in the fourth century C.E. He is the author of the *Abhidharmasamuccaya*, the foundational Mahayana text on the Abhidharma. The Bodhisattva Maitreya taught his five works to him, and Asanga transmitted these to the human world.

aspiring faith (*'dod pa'i dad pa*)
This is also known as longing faith. It is based on the desire to emulate.

bikshu (*dge slong*)
A fully ordained monk.

Birwapa or **Virupa** (*bir wa pa*)
An Indian Mahasiddha who received the Hevajra initiation directly from Vajra Nairatmya, the consort of the deity. He is known as Lord of Yogis. Originally he was the abbot of Nalanda University. Following his initiation by Vajra Nairatmya, he

attained six bhumis in six consecutive nights. He later left the monastery and lived as a yogi, performing many miraculous deeds.

bhumi (*sa*)

Bhumi means 'stage.' There are ten bhumis or stages on the arya bodhisattva's path to the ultimate enlightenment. The first bhumi is attained by the bodhisattva simultaneously with the path of seeing.

defilements (*nyon mongs*)

Emotions such as anger, pride, etc. which disturb the mind. The Sanskrit term, which is commonly used, is 'kleshas.'

dharani (*gzungs*)

This refers to mental retention, or to a short text containing mystical formulas, usually longer than a mantra.

Dharma (*chos*)

The term *chos* has ten major meanings in Tibetan: 1) phenomena; 2) spiritual path; 3) liberation or analytical cessation; 4) object of sixth consciousness; 5) teachings of the Buddhas; 6) life; 7) merit; 8) arisen from elements; 9) definite division; and 10) religious tradition or system.

eight branches of aryas' path, or **eightfold noble path** (*'phags lam gyi yan lag brgyad*)

This consists of: (1) right view; (2) right thought; (3) right speech; (4) right action; (5) right livelihood; (6) right effort; (7) right mindfulness; and (8) right concentration.

eight liberations (*rnam par thar pa brgyad*)

These are listed in *A Manual of Key Buddhist Terms*, by Lotsawa Kawa Paltseg (page 62).

eighteen spheres (*khams bco brgyad*)

Eighteen constituents or 'dhatus.' The six sense objects, the six senses and their six consciousnesses.

eightfold noble path

See eight branches of aryas' path.

five aggregates

See aggregates.

Five Buddha Families (*rigs lnga*)
Vairochana is associated with Buddha's body, Amitabha with Buddha's voice, Akshobya with Buddha's mind, Ratnasambhava with his spiritual qualities and Amoghasiddhi with his activities to benefit sentient beings.

five degenerations (*snyigs ma lnga*)
These degenerations appear progressively during degenerate times, when the teaching and practice of the Doctrine begin to decline: 1) shortening of life span; 2) amplification of defilements; 3) degeneration of sentient beings; 4) worsening of times; and 5) corruption of views.

Five Founding Masters of the Sakya tradition (*rje btsun gong ma lnga*)
Sachen Kunga Nyingpo (*sa chen kun dga' snying po*, 1092–1158); Sonam Tsemo (*rje btsun bsod nams rtse mo*, 1142–1182); Dakpa Gyaltsen (*rje btsun grags pa rgyal mtshan*, 1147–1216); Sakya Pandita Kunga Gyaltsen (*sa skya pandita kun dga' rgyal mtshan*, 1182–1251) and Drogon Chogyal Phagpa (*'gro mgon chos rgyal 'phags pa*, 1235–1280)

four noble truths (*'phags pa'i bden pa bzhi*)
They are: (1) the noble truth of suffering; (2) the noble truth of the origin of suffering; (3) the noble the truth of their cessation; and (4) the noble truth of the path leading to their cessation.

four correct endeavours (*yang dag spong ba bzhi*)
These are: (1) exerting effort not to generate nonvirtues not yet produced; (2) exerting effort to abandon nonvirtues already produced; (3) exerting effort to generate new virtues not already produced; and (4) exerting effort to maintain and develop the virtues which have been produced.

garuda (*klu za*)
Mythical bird like an eagle.

Gelug school (*dge lugs*)
The most recently founded and largest of the four school of Tibetan Buddhism, founded by Jetsun Tsong Khapa (1357–1419) in the fifteenth century.

Heaven of the Thirty-Three (*sum cu rtsa gsum gyi gnas*)
Celestial abode of one of the six classes of desire realm gods.

Hinayana (*theg dman*)

In terms of doctrine and tenets, the term Hinayana refers to the teachings of the 'lower vehicle,' or the lower two of the four Indian Buddhist tenets. In terms of causes and results, it refers to the paths and results of the shravakas and pratyekabuddhas.

Indra (*brgya byin*)

Indra, also known as Shakra, is the chief god of the desire realm. He resides on the summit of Mount Sumeru in the Palace of Complete Victory. He is one of the guardians of the ten directions.

Jain, Jainism (*rgyal ba pa*)

Indian ascetic school, whose adherents follow the teachings of Mahavira. One of the eternalist Hindu schools.

Kadampa (*bka' gdams*)

One of the sects of Tibetan Buddhist tradition, founded and brought to Tibet by Atisha (*jo bo rje*, 982–1054) which emphasized pure moral discipline and intense mind training in accordance with the *Prajnaparamitasutra*.

Kagyud (*bka' brgyud*)

One of the four principal schools of Tibetan Buddhism.

Kashyapa (*'od srung*)

The Buddha who appeared immediately prior to Buddha Shakyamuni.

King Trisong Deutsen (*khri srong lde'u bstan*)

The second great Dharma king of Tibet, eighth century.

Madhyamika school (*dbu ma pa*)

Literally, the 'Middle Way' school, which advocates a middle way, free from the extremes of nihilism and eternalism. This Mahayana philosophical school is considered to be the highest of the four Indian Buddhist schools. The second, lower Mahayana philosophical school is Cittamatrin (Yogachara or Mind-Only). The two Hinayana schools are Vaibashika and Sautrantika.

mahamudra (*phyag rgya chen po*)

Literally, 'the great seal.' A system of Vajrayana practice.